HOLY PLACES, HOLY PEOPLE

Helen

every blessing!

Gavin Wakefield

Alnmouth

GAVIN WAKEFIELD

Holy Places

HOLY PEOPLE

A Lion Book
an imprint of
Lion Hudson plc
Wilkinson House, Jordan Hill Road,
Oxford OX2 8DR, England
www.lionhudson.com
ISBN 978 0 7459 5304 5

First edition 2008
10 9 8 7 6 5 4 3 2 1 0

Acknowledgments
Illustrations by Julie Baines
Maps by Richard Watts (Total Media Services)
p.96: prayer from *2000 Years of Prayer*
(Canterbury Press, 2004)
p.107: prayer from *Methodist Worship Book*
(Methodist Publishing House, 1999)

A catalogue record for this book is available
from the British Library

This book has been printed on paper and board
independently certified as having been produced
from sustainable forests.

Typeset in 10.5/14pt Original Garamond
Printed and bound in Wales

CONTENTS

ACKNOWLEDGMENTS

Thanks to my careful and thoughtful readers, Fran Wakefield, Katharine Green, Kate Kirkpatrick and Julie Frederick. They have improved the text enormously.

I have benefited from conversations with many others who have sharpened my own thinking on the people discussed in the book and helped me with getting details sorted in my own mind – amongst them I am conscious that I must thank John Atherton, Alan Bartlett, Ian Bradley, Rosalind Brown, Stuart Cameron, Mark Cartledge, Brother Damian SSF, Nick Denham, Liz Hoare, John McManners, Ray Simpson, Ian Stockton and Kate Tristram.

FOREWORD

As a young friar back in the sixties I was quietly introduced to the church in the north-east of England and learned for the first time about the rich inheritance of this intriguing area. Northumberland then was mostly known as a gateway from the south into Scotland for holidaymakers and pilgrims alike. How things have changed!

Since then, much has been written commenting on and commending the early medieval church. The saints of Lindisfarne, with others who have exemplified what we now refer to as the Celtic church, have brought to a new generation an inspiration and a challenge to live the gospel with a renewed energy and vision.

But I have been waiting for something along the lines of this ordered and comprehensive directory, which not only reaches to the heart of the characters of Northumbria's golden age but also offers a practical guide as to how to go about discovering the treasures that are undoubtedly to be found here by the pilgrim traveller.

The numbers who visit the island of Lindisfarne are increasing annually. I am privileged to meet and talk with many who come (and return) with deep spiritual yearnings and who are seeking further knowledge and understanding of our heritage. This timely book will certainly help all who want to know more about the saints of the north-east.

Damian SSF, Vicar of Holy Island

The Places and the People

I was brought up in the south of England, but I have known the north-east for over thirty years, as a visitor and as a resident, and I have enjoyed its rich history, beautiful scenery and welcoming people. It is a part of England where history is visible in the stones of Hadrian's Wall, in the ancient churches at Hexham and at Escomb, and in the Anglo-Saxon settlement at Jarrow. These are set in a wonderful and varied landscape: from the rugged cliffs at Whitby to the golden sands of Bamburgh, and from the wild moors of the Pennines to the borderlands of the Cheviot Hills.

Here in the north-east people still celebrate their Christian heritage, most prominently in the stories of Aidan and Hilda, Cuthbert and Bede. In Weardale and Teesdale there are links to John Wesley and the earliest days of Methodism. Each year Durham Cathedral is packed for the Miners' Gala, as people continue to link their working lives with the Christian faith symbolized in that great building. In each holy place described here the story begun by holy people of previous generations is continued today.

It is that connection between past and present, with its gift for all our futures, that this guide brings to life. By learning something of the stories of the places and the people and how they responded to God, we can be encouraged in our own pilgrimage journeys.

We are fortunate to have a wonderful account of the origins of the English nation and its turn to Christianity in the history written by Bede in the eighth century. Bede was first and foremost a monk, but he is rightly celebrated as the first historian of the English people, and especially of their conversion from paganism to Christianity. He tells many stories of the early Christian missionaries in this region, and we will hear these as we make our own journey, whether on foot, in our car or in our imagination. Bede relates stories of Paulinus preaching at the royal hill camp of

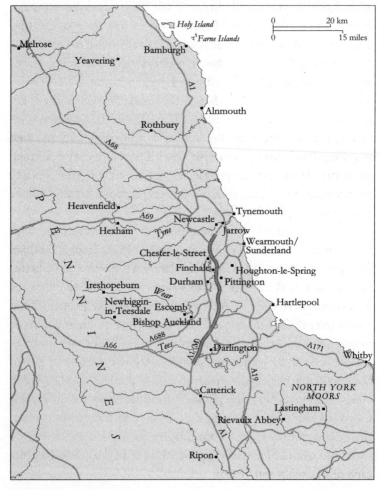

Yeavering, now near the Scottish border, and of Aidan establishing his monastery on Holy Island. So it makes sense to begin our pilgrimage in the north, and then to work our way southwards.

There are seven stages in the journey so that the guide can be used over the course of a week, but equally it can be used to help you in visiting places one by one, or by following along in your imagination as you read at home. Each 'Day' has four elements: People, Places, Prayer and Practicalities, along with some brief information about other places that you might like to visit.

The main focus is on the people who have made the places holy and important. Included are stories of famous and not-so-famous people, detailing what they achieved in their own day and how they speak to us today. The 'Places' section describes each site as a context for the stories of the holy people as well as giving details useful on a visit. Each Day has a prayer, linking us to the places and the people. If you are making the journey for yourself, the 'Practicalities' section provides some guidance about travelling to the places.

I have chosen the places that must be included because of their long-standing historic importance, such as Holy Island, Durham and Whitby. I have added in other places that deserve to be better known, such as Bamburgh, Monkwearmouth and Lastingham, for holy people have lived in these places too, and have shown what it means to seek God in the stuff of ordinary living. There is a short history that links the people and places together for you. In these places we hear the echoes of people who discovered the gift of holiness not in their own superhuman discipline but in the God in Christ who loves them deeply and utterly. In discovering this gift they took the risk of trusting that God in all things. As we visit these holy places – either in our imagination or in a physical sense – may the stories of these holy people lead us to the God who loves each of us deeply and utterly.

A Very Short History of Christianity in the North-east of England

This region was the most northerly frontier of the Roman empire, a fact set in the stones of that lengthy customs post known to us as Hadrian's Wall. It is likely that Christianity spread here early on, through traders and soldiers, but we have very little direct evidence. Even after Christianity was officially tolerated with the Edict of Milan in 313, the nearest known churches were at York to the south and Whithorn on the south-west coast of Scotland.

When the Roman empire departed in 410 the waves of pagan invaders forced Christianity into the north and west of Britain, and the kingdoms of the north-east became pagan. Initially there were two such kingdoms – Deira in the south, with its capital at York, and Bernicia in the north, with its capital at Bamburgh. It was not until the early seventh century that the spiritual tide turned in the north-east, with new missions from two directions.

First came the Roman mission, sent by Pope Gregory the Great and begun in the south of England under Archbishop Augustine. After a generation Bishop Paulinus was sent from Canterbury to be the chaplain for Queen Ethelberga of Kent when she married King Edwin at York. He was baptized there at Easter in 627, and York Minster is still on the site of the church that Edwin built. Paulinus' mission spread to Yeavering in Northumbria, and he also baptized many people at Catterick in Swaledale, the site of an ancient Roman fort on a major road.

However, Edwin was killed in battle in 633, and the Christians were attacked, many of them fleeing south. In the confusion that resulted the upper hand was won by Oswald, a member of a rival family. Oswald had been baptized on Iona whilst in exile, and after winning the battle of Heavenfield in 634 (see Day 2) he turned to Iona for missionaries, the second direction for mission. Thus came the godly man Aidan, who formed an Irish monastery on Lindisfarne. (It is now often known as Holy Island, though the names are used interchangeably; see Day 1.)

From Holy Island came many devout men – Chad and Cedd, Eata and Cuthbert – and the fabulous Lindisfarne Gospels, written by Eadfrith. Further Christian communities were formed, the best known being Whitby (see Day 7), founded by Hilda. (More detailed information about the Synod of Whitby is in the Appendix at the back of the book.) Other important places at this time were Hexham (see Day 2), under Wilfrid, and Wearmouth-Jarrow, founded by Benedict Biscop (see Day 3). At the beginning of the eighth century Bede began to write the story of the conversion of the English, and so we know delightful details about some of these people. Disaster struck in 793, with the first Viking raid on the English mainland on the monastery at Lindisfarne. The monks did not disperse at once but eventually they had to leave, and they re-formed their Community of St Cuthbert at Chester-le-Street in 883. At the same time there was a steady flow of pastoral work and preaching, as small churches were created and monasteries developed.

In 995 in a decisive move the Community of St Cuthbert relocated to Durham. Their cathedral was torn down by the Normans a century later, and they replaced it with the massive cathedral that still stands in Durham (see Day 5). The shrine of Cuthbert became very rich and the monks of Durham very powerful through the region. In this period the organization of the church was overhauled and parishes were systematically created so that everyone was part of the structure, at least in theory. Monastic communities such as that at Durham now came to follow the Benedictine Rule, the monastic guidelines drawn up by St Benedict in the sixth century and gradually adopted as the standard Rule of Life for monasteries in Western Europe. Benedictine monasteries were formed again at the ancient sites, such as Whitby, Jarrow and Holy Island. The bishops of Durham were important landowners, holding the territory for the king, against the Scots. They could mint their own money, and at times they raised armies; no wonder they became known as prince-bishops.

At the Reformation in the sixteenth century the shrine of Cuthbert lost its jewels as well as the Lindisfarne Gospels, a very unpopular move locally. Many people joined the Pilgrimage of Grace in 1536 to protest about the changes to the familiar services and ways of the church. Inevitably there was a crackdown from the authorities, but from 1530 to 1559 Bishop Cuthbert Tunstall steered a careful path under Henry VIII, Mary Tudor and Elizabeth; in all that time there were no serious persecutions, and certainly no burnings. Tunstall's peaceable middle way was lived out in the ministry of his great-nephew, Bernard Gilpin, an energetic priest at Houghton-le-Spring (see Day 4).

In the centuries that followed, County Durham and Newcastle were at the heart of the Industrial Revolution, with coal mining, steel making, railways and shipbuilding all important; indeed the first passenger railway in the world ran here from Stockton to Darlington. Given this change it is not surprising that renewal movements in Christianity also found a home: Presbyterians and Quakers were strong in the seventeenth century, whilst Methodism under John and Charles Wesley and their many successors was especially strong in the eighteenth and nineteenth centuries (see Day 6). In the twentieth century the Pentecostal Movement began in Britain in Sunderland, inspired by the local vicar, Alexander Boddy (see Day 3).

Today Christianity is once again seen as one religion amongst many, yet here in the north-east people still value their Christian heritage, even if their church attendance is erratic – this was the English region with the highest proportion of self-identified Christians in the 2001 Census. The holy places in this history and on this pilgrimage continue to be places of worship and encouragement for many people today.

TIMELINE

This timeline is intended to list the key events included in the stories told in this guide. A full list of the events in the lives of the people described would require many more entries. A number of dates are approximate, especially those before 1100.

100	c.122–33	Hadrian's Wall built
300	313	Edict of Milan brings official toleration of Christianity in the Roman empire
	c.380	St Ninian at Whithorn
400	410	Roman rule in Britain abandoned
500	c.563	Columba goes to Iona
	593	Bernicia and Deira united as Northumbria through marriage
	597	Death of Columba on Iona
600	616	Edwin becomes King of Northumbria
	627	Baptism of Edwin and Hilda by Paulinus
	633	Death of Edwin in battle
	634	Battle of Heavenfield
		Oswald becomes King of Northumbria
	635	Aidan sent to Lindisfarne
	642	Death of Oswald in battle
		Oswy becomes King of Northumbria (died 670)
	647	Founding of monastery at Hartlepool
	651	Death of Aidan at Bamburgh
	657	Whitby monastery founded by Hilda
	661	Colman becomes Bishop of Lindisfarne
	664	Synod of Whitby
		Death of Cedd in Lastingham
	665	Consecration of Wilfrid as bishop
	672	Hexham Abbey founded by Wilfrid
	674	Wearmouth monastery founded by Benedict Biscop
	680	Death of Hilda (born c. 614)
	681	Jarrow monastery founded
	685	Consecration of Cuthbert as bishop
	687	Death of Cuthbert (born c. 634)
	689	Death of Benedict Biscop (born 628)
700	709	Death of Wilfrid (born c. 634)
	715–21	Probable date for the production of Lindisfarne Gospels
	716	Death of Ceolfrith (born 642)

	721	Death of Eadfrith
	731	Publication of Bede's *Ecclesiastical History*
	735	Death of Bede (born c. 673)
	793	First Viking raid on Lindisfarne
800	875	Final Viking raids on Lindisfarne
	883	Community of St Cuthbert settled at Chester-le-Street
900	995	Community of St Cuthbert moved to Durham
	999	First cathedral at Durham ready for Cuthbert's shrine
1000	1066	Norman invasion of England
	1069	Harrowing of the North (Yorkshire)
	1083	Benedictine monastery at Durham replaces the old community
	c.1087	Death of Reinfrid at Whitby
	1093	New cathedral at Durham begun
		Death of Queen Margaret of Scotland (born 1046)
1100	1104	Translation of Cuthbert's body to the new Durham cathedral
	c.1110	Symeon of Durham writes *Libellus de Exordio*
	1133	Completion of first phase of the cathedral
	1170	Death of Godric (born c. 1065)
1500	1536	Pilgrimage of Grace
	1539/41	Dissolution of the monastery at Durham
	1556	Bernard Gilpin becomes Rector of Easington and Archdeacon of Durham, becoming Rector of Houghton-le-Spring the following year
	1569	Rising in the north
	1583	Death of Bernard Gilpin (born 1517)
1600	1692	London Lead Company established in Middleton-in-Teesdale by Quakers
1700		Rise of Methodism
	1742	First visit by John Wesley to Newcastle
		Many subsequent visits by both John and Charles Wesley
	1784	Death of Jacob Rowell
	1791	Death of John Wesley (born 1703)
1800	1802	Death of Christopher Hopper (born 1722)
	1820s	Coal mining greatly expanded with development of East Durham coalfield
1900	c.1900	Sunderland said to be the largest shipbuilding town in the world
	1908–14	Pentecostal revival begun in Sunderland
	1928	Death of Mary Boddy (born 1855)
	1930	Death of Alexander Boddy (born 1854)

DAY 1

Holy Island:
Cradle of Faith

The pilgrimage begins on Holy Island, the home of the first successful Christian mission in north-east England. Here Aidan founded his first English monastery, and from here many monks and priests went to share the gospel for more than two centuries. This is the place where the Lindisfarne Gospels were lovingly written and illustrated, and where pilgrims came to pray at the tomb of Cuthbert, in the hope of healing and other blessings. The life of prayer was renewed in the eleventh century in the new Benedictine monastery and continues today in the parish church and other centres on the island.

Holy Island is much loved and visited for reasons besides its spiritual pull, including Lindisfarne Castle in its dramatic setting on Beblowe Rock and the profusion of bird life in the National Nature Reserve. The tidal nature of the crossing is essential to the appeal of the island, creating a rhythm of existence that we cannot escape: connected to the mainland, then separated for a time. As a part-time island Lindisfarne embodies a rhythm for living that is all too easily lost in a world that thinks it wants to be 24/7.

The holy people described in this Day are the founder of the monastery, Aidan; his famous successor, Cuthbert, hermit, bishop and miracle-worker; and the later bishop and abbot, Eadfrith, who wrote and illustrated the Lindisfarne Gospels. The holy places are St Mary's Church, Lindisfarne Priory and the island itself.

People

Aidan (died 651)

Aidan is rightly remembered as the holy founder of the Irish mission to Northumbria, and there are many stories of his life and work in this part of the world. We know very little about his background, though it is likely that he was from a noble family, as was the case with other church leaders of the time. He may even have been related to Columba (the founder of Iona), since the monastery on Iona was a family affair, with many of the abbots in its first 100 years belonging to Columba's family.

We begin to learn about Aidan after the success of Oswald at the battle of Heavenfield in 634 (see Day 2). Wanting to create a Christian kingdom, Oswald turned to Iona for missionaries. The monastery first sent a priest called Corman, a man of 'austere disposition', and he did not go down very well with the English. His sermons were overlong and he returned to Iona despondent, complaining that the English were an 'ungovernable people of an obstinate and barbarous temperament'.

It was at the consequent consultation that the Irish monk Aidan stood up and said:

'Brother, it seems to me that you were too severe on your ignorant hearers. You should have followed the practice of the Apostles, and begun by giving them the milk of simpler teaching, and gradually nourished them with the word of God.' (Bede, Ecclesiastical History, *Book 3, Chapter 5)*

Aidan's wisdom was recognized; he was consecrated bishop, and with twelve companion monks was sent to Northumbria with their blessing. Aidan met King Oswald at the royal base of Bamburgh. Oswald hoped that Aidan would make his own base there, but Aidan was concerned about being too close to the king. Instead he accepted the gift of Lindisfarne from Oswald. This was an ideal location: as a small island it held reminiscences of Iona, and Bamburgh was in sight and was easily reached by boat.

A remarkable partnership developed between the warrior king and the missionary bishop: Aidan's command of Anglo-Saxon was not great, and the king himself would sometimes act as his interpreter, having learned the Irish language during his stay on Iona. Over time other priests and monks from Iona joined Aidan, and, under his leadership, baptized people and built new churches and monasteries.

Our only record of Aidan comes from Bede, who gives a very positive impression. This may have had something to do with Bede's desire to promote a careful following of the monastic life in his own day. Nonetheless he chose to do this with the example of a man from a tribe different from his own, and from a somewhat different church tradition, which had an erroneous way of dating Easter as far as Bede was concerned.

As Bede puts it in Book 3, Chapter 5, of his *Ecclesiastical History*:

'... the highest recommendation of his teaching to all was that he and his followers lived as they taught. He never sought or cared for any worldly possessions, and loved to give away to the poor who chanced to meet him whatever he received from kings or wealthy folk. Whether in town or country, he always travelled on foot unless compelled by necessity to ride; and whatever people he met on his walks, whether high or low, he stopped and spoke to them. If they were heathen, he urged them to be baptized; and if they were Christians, he strengthened their faith, and inspired them by word and deed to live a good life and to be generous to others.'

Aidan had an enormous impact on people through the manner of his life, which was consistent with his teaching. I have identified four of the most notable characteristics of his work and holiness here:

1. *His passion for God*

Aidan's spiritual work was at the centre of his being. As a monk he was committed to regular prayers, reading Scripture and saying the Psalms. Much of this was done from memory; as he walked around Oswald's kingdom he would get his companions to join him in learning the Psalms and other parts of the Bible.

He had learned from Iona that before building a monastery monks should pray and fast on the site for forty days and nights. This they did on Lindisfarne despite the pressing need for shelter, and he passed on this lesson to his followers, so that Cedd spent forty days and nights in prayer and spiritual battle before building the monastery at Lastingham (see Day 7). For Aidan and his followers, holiness began in prayer and total commitment to God.

2. *People before possessions*

Aidan was prepared to accept possessions – for example, in receiving graciously Oswald's gifts for the monastery – but possessions were not to get in the way of following Christ's example and encountering Christ in others. One of the best-known and best-loved stories about Aidan illustrates this.

Aidan had determined to travel the kingdom by foot, as he knew this gave him a better relationship with the ordinary people. It was kings and their warriors who owned horses and this put them literally above other folks. But King Oswin, successor to Oswald in the southern kingdom of Deira, insisted on giving Aidan a fine horse, so that he could get about more quickly on urgent business. As Aidan had anticipated, this distanced him from ordinary people. So, when a beggar asked for alms from this apparently rich horseman, he received more than he had expected: for Aidan dismounted and gave him the king's horse, complete with its fine saddle and all the trappings that Oswin had given him. Oswin rebuked Aidan, but the saint was ready: 'Which is more valuable, the child of a mare or the child of God?' Perhaps we will be surprised to learn that the king accepted Aidan's criticism and promised not to interfere with his generosity to those in need. Aidan himself was deeply moved by the king's humility, and realized that such a king would not live long.

In this story we have a prime example of Aidan's ability to hold light to possessions, as well as his own sense of humility and equality of persons. This takes us to the third point.

3. Encouragement and gentle authority
As we read Bede's accounts of holy people it is easy at first to confuse the different characters, and to form a general impression of holy people who went around praying, doing good and performing miracles. As we read on and distinguish the individuals more fully, so their different characteristics emerge. For example, whilst Cuthbert has many healing miracles attributed to him, Aidan has none, but rather two nature miracles: the calming of a storm and the shifting of a wind to protect Bamburgh from fire caused by an enemy.

So when we read that amongst other virtues Aidan 'cultivated peace and love', that 'he was above anger and greed', and that 'he used his priestly authority to check the proud and powerful', we may have some confidence in what Bede tells us. The story of Aidan giving away Oswin's horse is a powerful illustration of all these good qualities.

Another story illustrates Aidan's ability to encourage even the most powerful of kings without sycophancy. One Easter Day there was a great meal for the king and his bishop. They were about to start a rich feast served on silver dishes, when a servant came in, speaking of the hungry crowd outside begging for alms. Immediately Oswald sent his own food outside for the people and ordered the silver dish to be cut up so they could buy more. Aidan praised the king's generosity, taking his hand and exclaiming, 'May this hand never wither with age.' The story was partly an explanation for the relic of Oswald's hand and arm held in Bamburgh in Bede's day, but it also highlights the mutual regard of the two men and their shared values in caring for the poor on the basis of their Christian faith.

This story highlights the importance of encouraging other people in Christ-like behaviour. Here was Aidan strengthening the king's resolve as a Christian, and thereby setting an example for other people in their discipleship. That support of course drew its power from Aidan's own example of holy living. Another important example of Aidan's encouragement is found in the story of Hilda (see Day 7).

4. *The importance of Christian education*

Aidan was aware of the need to have a long-term plan for the nurturing of the Christian faith, and he reminds us that holiness is not just about spontaneous acts of love and mercy. Throughout the kingdom, he set up small monasteries as mission stations and schools. This was very important for the long-term future of the church, for he did not rely on bringing in priests and monks from Iona, but took in local lads to learn the faith, through a form of one-to-one mentoring.

The most important school was that on Lindisfarne itself. It was a living demonstration of the way that the gospel breaks down barriers. Aidan was known for using gifts of money in ways that surprised onlookers. One day he caused a stir by buying a slave in the local market, and then freeing him. The man was so grateful that he would not leave Aidan, and eventually the freed man was admitted to the monastery school to train for the priesthood. This was a school that took in both noble-born (Wilfrid; see Day 2) and ex-slaves, and taught them together in humble surroundings. The school took seriously the need to train local men to be the missionaries and priests to their own people, whether high-born or low.

Aidan used the monastic tradition of education to build the future of the church, by training many future priests, bishops and missionaries, and by doing it in accordance with what he understood to be gospel values. Such practical holiness, united to his gentle but strong character, gave the church in Northumbria the foundation for its subsequent achievements, which we will learn about on this pilgrimage journey.

Aidan's death came on 31 August 651, just eleven days after the murder of the humble King Oswin. It is not hard to imagine that the shock of the news may have contributed to his death. He died by the church at Bamburgh, leaning on a wooden beam, which is said to be preserved in the building. He was buried by his brothers in the monks' cemetery on Holy Island, though after the Synod of Whitby (664) his bones were separated, some being returned to Iona and others left on Lindisfarne. They are believed to have been placed later in Cuthbert's coffin and so eventually found a resting place in Durham Cathedral.

Cuthbert (634–87)

Though Aidan and Cuthbert lived in the same area and their lives overlapped we have no record of them ever meeting. The only connection we hear of is that on the night of Aidan's death in 651, the teenage Cuthbert was out watching the sheep on the hills above Melrose when he saw a great light going into the sky that he believed to be a holy soul being received into heaven. The next morning, on hearing that Aidan had died, he took this as a sign that he should enter the monastic life and presented himself at Melrose.

We are fortunate in having three accounts of Cuthbert's life, all written shortly after his death. The first was written anonymously by a monk of Lindisfarne; the second was written by Bede, in verse; and the third, a prose life, was also written by Bede. Both writers have material from eyewitnesses, giving us a uniquely detailed picture of a life from this period, though they were not always interested in the same details as we are, offering more on his miraculous deeds and his death than, say, the content of his preaching or the organization of the monasteries in which he lived. The level of detail means that this account does not try to cover everything we know about Cuthbert, but seeks to make sense of his career and explain why he was considered holy.

Cuthbert arrived at Melrose on horseback, accompanied by a servant and carrying his spear: he was another person of noble birth who was offering his life to God in this religion new to his people. He was received by the prior Boisil, until the abbot Eata arrived; Eata was one of the first group of twelve boys who studied under Aidan. In his turn Cuthbert now studied the Scriptures and trained as a monk in the Irish tradition under the guidance of these two men. He was deeply committed in observing the Rule of the community, abstaining from alcohol and fasting regularly, though not so drastically that he could not stay fit and strong enough to do his physical work.

A few years later, around 663, the monastery was granted land by King Alchfrith, son of King Oswy, for a new monastery at Ripon. Eata led twelve monks first to pray for and then to build the new monastery. Cuthbert was amongst those sent, and he was appointed to the important role of guestmaster, which involved caring for travellers who called at the monastery for help. This venture lasted only a short time, for Eata was unwilling to accept the Roman customs desired by Alchfrith. They returned to Melrose, whilst the site at Ripon was passed on to Wilfrid (see Day 2).

On returning to Melrose Cuthbert was afflicted by a plague that was spreading through the country. His brothers prayed through the night for him, desperate to keep this holy man with them. Cuthbert did recover but he was left weakened for the rest of his life. Boisil also caught the plague and died after a week, a week in which he and Cuthbert studied the Gospel of John, and Boisil spoke prophetic words about the future of Abbot Eata and of Cuthbert.

On the death of his mentor Cuthbert, still in his mid-twenties, was made prior. He used this post not just to encourage the monks but also to tour the countryside preaching the gospel, and he became known for performing miraculous healings and for his devotion in celebrating the Mass. Like the Irish monks before him Cuthbert was prepared to go to the poorest places to be with peasants who would otherwise not hear of the love of God in Christ. At times he would live amongst the rough hill folk, realizing the need to strengthen their faith at testing times, for they would all too easily turn back to incantations and amulets to deal with illness. In this context of disease and a return to pagan ways perhaps we understand better the importance of the healing and exorcism miracles attributed to Cuthbert, a sign of the power of God at work in him.

After the Synod of Whitby (see Appendix) Eata became abbot and then also Bishop of Lindisfarne and he took Cuthbert with him as prior. The community was not united, for some did not keep the Rule as Cuthbert wished, and it took time for him to win them over by example, patience and persistence. He continued his custom of visiting outside the monastery, still preaching, healing and exorcizing. His wisdom and love were such that people would confess their sins to him and he would find himself weeping in penitence with them. Such empathy helps to explain the love that people felt for this holy man.

Although noted for his very public ministry Cuthbert also felt called to a deep prayer life, and he would go without sleep in order to pray. In the course of time this became a calling to the hermit life, extending the example of Aidan and Columba, who both heard a call to go out to the people and to withdraw to pray. Cuthbert found the right locations on the same islands as Aidan: first Hobthrush, or St Cuthbert's Isle, off Lindisfarne and then on the Inner Farne island near Bamburgh, where he built a simple room and oratory for prayer. Here he was to focus on prayer, engaging in spiritual battle on behalf of the people. The brothers from Lindisfarne did offer some support, but gradually he withdrew more and more and it seems he spent some years in this life of prayer.

He was not alone in the strict sense, for besides visits from his brother monks, his reputation for holiness had grown so that people would come to him for prayer and counsel. His holiness was seen in the many miracles associated with him, both whilst travelling and at his hermitage. He was perceived to have power over nature: Bede recounts tales of an eagle serving him by dropping a fish and on another occasion a raven bringing an offering of pig's lard. On his hermitage on the Inner Farne he apparently grew a rich crop of barley after its proper season. He is famous for praying all night in the sea; in one incident Cuthbert was visiting the monastery at Coldingham and in the morning was spotted by one of the monks having his feet warmed and dried by a pair of otters. In other miracles he put out a fire in the house of his old nurse by praying, causing the wind to change direction, and he performed miracles of healing, witnessed by people who told their stories directly to Bede.

Cuthbert's austerity was not secret but lived out very close to the royal centre of Bamburgh. By this stage Northumbria was ruled by King Ecgfrith, a younger son of Oswy, much troubled as a ruler and as a man, and capable of murder and aggression verging on genocide. The sight of Cuthbert's hermitage so near to the royal fortress may well have acted as a rebuke, for in contemporary Irish law the ultimate weapon in seeking justice was a hunger strike at the door of the offender.

Nonetheless Ecgfrith desired that Cuthbert be bishop in his kingdom, and at a synod at Twyford (probably modern-day Alnmouth) he was elected as Bishop of Hexham. Much persuasion was required from the king, Bishop Trumwine of the Picts, and brethren from Lindisfarne until Cuthbert reluctantly gave way. His consecration at York was delayed until the following Easter (685), and an exchange was negotiated with Eata, so that Cuthbert could be Bishop of Lindisfarne and Eata could go to the newer bishopric of Hexham. As bishop Cuthbert returned to his itinerant ministry, still living frugally, whilst encouraging people in their faith and bringing healing where he could.

His time as bishop was less than two years and he sensed his death coming close. After Christmas 686 he returned to the Inner Farne, desiring to be alone. His death, after so many privations in life, was not easy. In the anonymous life his death is described in peaceful enough terms: 'Being attracted by the love of his former solitary life he returned to the island... He remained alone, satisfied with the conversation and ministry of angels.' A hint of harshness is provided by an allusion to Mark 1:13, which speaks of the angels ministering to Jesus in the wilderness of temptation.

Bede was willing to be more explicit, drawing on the testimony of the monk Herefrith, who had been with Cuthbert at the very end of his life. Herefrith told how Cuthbert had been left alone for days on the Inner Farne in a dreadful storm, which prevented Herefrith from returning. When he did get back he found Cuthbert had been without food or drink, and his face was marked with agony, suffering a dreadful sore.

This may give us a clue as to how Cuthbert saw this island hermitage, not as a beautiful private sanctuary, but as a desert-like place in which he encountered God in a deep way. It took the insight of Bede to relate Cuthbert's ending to that of Christ with a quote from the book of Lamentations: 'It is good for a man to have borne the yoke in his youth; he shall sit in solitude and be silent, because he will raise himself above himself' (3:27–28; quoted in Bede). This sentence, used in the monastic liturgy for Holy Saturday, is the context for Bede's telling of Cuthbert's story, for it is found in the opening lines of his prose life. It is as though Bede sees Cuthbert's life and especially his difficult death as identifying him with Christ on the cross. In his death on the Inner Farne, to us a nature reserve, Cuthbert is not a busy bishop trying to find peace and quiet, but a man battling with the spiritual forces of evil, and ultimately a man crucified with Christ, alone and in the darkness.

Cuthbert's evident holiness and popularity in his lifetime meant that his brothers did not bury his body in solitude on the Inner Farne as Cuthbert had originally wished, but instead they took him to their church on Lindisfarne for burial. Almost immediately miracle stories were being told, and as Cuthbert had feared the shrine became popular and led to increasing wealth for the monastery. In 698, on the anniversary of his death, his coffin was opened for the reinterring of his bones as relics. A further miracle was detected in the preservation of Cuthbert's body and the brightness of his vestments. A new tomb was therefore built for the increased flow of pilgrims, and around 715 the Lindisfarne Gospels were created by Bishop Eadfrith in Cuthbert's honour.

Cuthbert's story as told by Bede and the anonymous monk is physically and spiritually demanding but relatively straightforward: an able young man has a vision; he becomes an exemplary monk; he soon shows his ability as preacher, miracle worker and counsellor; he works his way through the ranks, maintaining his integrity; he finds a place to pray alone; and he ends as a much-loved bishop. There is truth in this version, but in seeking to learn from Cuthbert's holiness of life we should also take account of the complications of power and wealth. Cuthbert needed to work with the most powerful dynasty in Britain and with the aristocracy of his day. Many of his miracles are associated with the leading members of society, and in order to maintain his place after the Synod of Whitby he needed to accept the decision of King Oswy to follow Roman practice. Like Aidan he had to negotiate a narrow pathway between simply doing the king's bidding and antagonizing the rulers on whose goodwill his mission depended. One suspects this took considerable thought and skill, as well as courage.

Cuthbert's concern about the lure of money may well have been sharpened by the considerable wealth being given to establish the church – wealth often generated by the conquest of other tribes. Whilst there is no reason to doubt his personal poverty the evidence of wealth bestowed on the church is still visible in his pectoral cross on show in Durham Cathedral, which has housed his remains for more than a thousand years (see Day 5). The making of the Lindisfarne Gospels is further evidence of the disposable income available to the community on Lindisfarne.

These comments are not intended to denigrate Cuthbert's character and achievements; they are to remember that holiness may be described in straightforward ways, but has to be lived out in complex and difficult circumstances. Like the other people mentioned in this guide Cuthbert had to live with the temptations of power and wealth, precisely because of the success of the Northumbrian kings in battle and the growth of the church in the kingdom. It makes his perseverance in such an exemplary lifestyle all the more striking.

Eadfrith (died 721) and the Lindisfarne Gospels

Although the original Lindisfarne Gospels have survived to the present day we have to acknowledge that we cannot be certain about where they were written, who was responsible or when exactly they were produced. Scholars continue to debate these and many other details. In what follows I am relying on the work of Michelle Brown, former Curator of Illuminated Manuscripts at The British Library and the foremost expert on the Lindisfarne Gospels.

Given the reputation scholars sometimes have for overturning popular stories it may come as a surprise to learn that Dr Brown argues forcibly that this gospel book was indeed produced on Lindisfarne, by Bishop Eadfrith, as stated in a much later comment, and most likely in the period 715–21, as the shrine and cult of St Cuthbert developed.

Eadfrith had possibly known Cuthbert personally, for he was a senior priest and monk of the Lindisfarne monastery at the time of the opening of Cuthbert's tomb in 698. Indeed, when Cuthbert's successor as bishop, Eadbert, died in May 698 Eadfrith was appointed as the new bishop. Eadfrith seems to have been the key figure in developing the cult of Cuthbert, for he commissioned the unknown monk of Lindisfarne to write the first *Life of Cuthbert* around 705, and Bede to write a second prose *Life* just before his death in 721; both these works were dedicated to Eadfrith.

Further information about Eadfrith comes from an addition made to the Lindisfarne Gospels in the mid-900s, the colophon of Aldred, a priest of the Community of St Cuthbert during its time at Chester-le-Street (see Day 4). Whilst added more than 200 years after the production of the Gospels its statement that 'Eadfrith originally wrote this book' is considered to be accurate. It seems that Eadfrith himself was the handwriter and the illuminator of the entire book – a remarkable feat of endurance even if it had not been such an artistic masterpiece.

Eadfrith brought together ideas and decoration from all the sources one can imagine at that time: Irish, Pictish, Germanic, Anglo-Saxon, Roman, Byzantine and Coptic. Lindisfarne was not a remote hermitage but an integral part of European culture, and we know that Eadfrith collaborated with Bede, the pre-eminent scholar of his day, on other projects – if Lindisfarne did not have its own extensive library then one of the best in Europe was not far away in Bede's monastery of Wearmouth-Jarrow. Eadfrith must have closely observed both art and the natural world, for many birds of Lindisfarne can be identified in the decorations.

The exhibition in the Heritage Centre offers an excellent introduction to the Lindisfarne Gospels.

PLACES

St Mary's Church

St Mary's Church is in the south-west corner of the island, close to the site of Aidan's first wooden church, Bishop Finan's second wooden church of St Peter and the stone church built a generation later by their Anglo-Saxon successors. The present building dates from the twelfth century, when Lindisfarne Priory was re-established by the Benedictine monks of Durham Cathedral. The oldest wall is the east wall above the chancel arch. The line of a Saxon curved arch is visible and above it a small Saxon door, possibly evidence of the use of the building by the first Benedictine monks. During the thirteenth century the building was extended to its present size.

This is the parish church of the island, and prayer is offered daily, morning and evening, for the island, its visitors and the world. The building contains many reminders of its present use and the history of the island. The entrance has recently been opened up in an attractive manner, and an open space has been created around the font. In this west end there are modern stained-glass windows of Aidan and Cuthbert.

Facing down the church is the ancient chancel arch with the sanctuary beyond it. In the south aisle on the right is the powerful sculpture *The Journey* cut in elm by Fenwick Lawson. It depicts six monks carrying the coffin of Cuthbert on its long journey from Lindisfarne, which started after Viking raids and ended in Durham. The sculptor writes:

'... *the idea of movement, inherent in the journey itself, is a main factor in the formal concern of the sculpture: the movement expressed in each of the six figures; the movement in the different attitudes of the heads; the implied movement in, and between, the unfinished/finished heads, suggesting a movement in time'.*

Just beyond the sculpture is a case with a reproduction of the Lindisfarne Gospels, which were written here.

In the north aisle on the other side of the church there is a modern reproduction of Cuthbert's coffin, showing the details of the drawings, which include apostles, archangels and angels and the saint surrounded by the symbols of the four Gospel writers. Here too is the Fishermen's Chapel, a place to remember the island's fishermen as well as the fishermen called by Jesus, a scene depicted in the window here. The intricately worked carpet was made by local women and is based on the Lindisfarne Gospel carpet page for St Luke's Gospel.

From the sanctuary the oldest wall of the present church can be seen above the chancel arch. In the sanctuary itself are more items to remind today's pilgrims of the story of this place. On the floor is a second carpet page, this time from St Mark's Gospel. Behind the altar is a reredos illuminated with the crucifixion and the traditional figures of Mary the mother of Jesus and the apostle John; around them are saints connected to the island. From the top left: Cuthbert, the bishop and hermit; Aidan the founder of Lindisfarne; Wilfrid, who was trained here (see Day 2); and Columba, who founded Iona. From the bottom left: Oswald, who gave the land for the monastery (see Day 2); Mary; John; and Bede, the historian (see Day 3). On the north wall by the communion rail is a small but significant present from the diocese of Nidaros in Norway, given in 1993 – a bust of their first Christian king

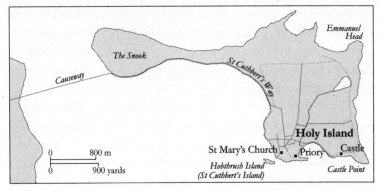

and a letter of apology for the first Viking raid in Europe, on Lindisfarne in 793.

If you are visiting but are not able to join others in prayer here why not stop for a moment and give thanks for the holy people who dedicated their lives to God in this holy place. Near the door there is a board on which you can leave your own prayer requests to be included in the prayers that evening.

Lindisfarne Priory

Next door to the church are the ruins of the twelfth-century priory – the remains of a daughter house run by Durham Cathedral after the Norman Conquest of 1066 (see Day 5). By that time Lindisfarne was not a major centre; monks seemed to regard a posting to Holy Island as one they would rather avoid, and the community was never large. The site is now under the care of English Heritage and is well worth a visit to see how a monastery was organized in the later medieval period, always remembering that this was not how Aidan arranged or built his monastery.

The rest of Holy Island

A short distance away from the church and the priory ruins is the marketplace. The probable extent of the inner sanctum is shown by a *vallum*, an earthen bank that symbolized the boundary between the most sacred part of the settlement and the rest. The outer section of the first monastery, with domestic and industrial activity, may have extended to Marygate, the present high street.

Hobthrush or St Cuthbert's Isle is a significant spot off the south-west tip of the island. An Irish monastery was not only a place of quiet contemplation, but also a busy mission centre, school, hospital and home to many people. For that reason Aidan and later Cuthbert and their successors would use Hobthrush Isle as a place for personal prayers away from the crowds. The island can be reached at low tide by walking over the rocks with the outline of a small chapel in sight. With the wind blowing, the sea washing around you, the birds and seals singing, it is a place for contemplation of creation and the creator. A few minutes here is refreshing; the hours Aidan and Cuthbert spent here, sometimes with the tide in, were more demanding spiritual work.

The ridge on the south side of the priory is called the Heugh. A steep but short climb to the look-out point offers views over the village and over the sea to Bamburgh. There may have been stone crosses on the Heugh in the Anglo-Saxon period as part of a pilgrim way.

The village is on the likely site of the early monastery, which explains the scarcity of archaeological evidence, but there are modern aids to pilgrims. Amongst these are the Gospel Garden, the Heritage Centre, with a most detailed reproduction of the Lindisfarne Gospels, the Open Gate house of the Community of Aidan and Hilda, and the Lindisfarne Scriptorium, where Mary Fleeson produces contemporary versions of decorated pages.

To the east of Marygate lies the harbour, now smaller than in Aidan's day. It is still used by the local fishermen, though today they are significantly fewer in number. In the seventh century this would have been a busy place, allowing access to the monastery and possibly serving as the base for the warships of the Northumbrian king. The castle is ahead and this pathway is often thronged with visitors. Yet even on the busiest days it is possible to find quiet spots by walking past the castle onto the east shore and the north shore. A relatively short walk offers a space to be still, perhaps to watch the wonderful bird life, to let the beauty of the coast renew you, or to reflect on the holy lives that have made this the Holy Island of Lindisfarne.

Prayer

God of sea, God of sky,
God of wind, God of waves,
God of us all in creation,

Thank you for this holy place,
    which speaks through its beauty and rawness.
Thank you for its holy people,
    who point us to Jesus the Holy One of God.

Strengthen us to be holy people in the places to which you take us.

Practicalities

Holy Island
Holy Island is reached from the A1, about 6 miles south of Berwick. The road crosses a causeway, which is covered by the tide twice a day. It is very important to check tide times for safe crossings and to obey the times given.
http://www.lindisfarne.org.uk/

Once on the island drive to the public car park on the edge of the village. All the sites are signed from there. Refreshments of various kinds are available at several places in the village.

The medieval priory is open every day, except at Christmas and on New Year's Day. Check the website for details: *http://www.english-heritage.org.uk/server/show/nav.13257*

St Mary's Church is open every day, beginning with services of Morning Prayer at 7.30 a.m. and Holy Communion at 8 a.m., and ending with Evening Prayer at 5.30 p.m. *http://www.lindisfarne.org.uk/religion/david1.htm*

If you are feeling energetic you can walk the 97-mile St Oswald's Way, starting on Holy Island and taking in Bamburgh and Alnmouth, before ending at Heavenfield (see Day 2). The walk can easily be extended the 5 miles into Hexham.

Other places

A visit to Holy Island is likely to take a whole day and many visitors stay longer. There are more places in the vicinity associated with the saints discussed, and here they are mentioned very briefly, roughly from north to south.

Melrose: The present abbey ruins date from the twelfth century onwards; the Anglo-Saxon monastery is on private land at Old Melrose below Scott's View.

St Cuthbert's Church, Norham: St Cuthbert's Church is an important resting place for Cuthbert's body on the community's journey of 875–83.

Yeavering: The site at Yeavering includes a hill fort that was a royal centre for kings of Bernicia and, at its foot, the River Glen, where Paulinus baptized many people over a 36-day period.

Cuthbert's Cave, near Chatton: This cave is at the base of a hill that looks back to Holy Island. It is said to be the place where

Cuthbert's coffin was first brought from the island after the Viking raids. It is on the St Cuthbert's Way and is well signed from minor roads. There is a walk of nearly a mile from the car park.

St Aidan's Church, Bamburgh: Aidan built a church here outside the royal fortress at the beginning of his work in Northumbria in 635. He died on this spot in 651, leaning against a wooden beam reputedly preserved in the church.

St Cuthbert's Chapel, Inner Farne: The Farne Islands can be visited by boat from Seahouses. Aidan was the first hermit to live here, but Cuthbert lived on this island for many years, building himself a hut and chapel. Others followed his example after his death. The chapel seen today was built in 1370 by Benedictine monks from Durham. A landing fee is payable to the National Trust for Inner Farne, and wearing a hat is useful during the spring to protect you from the birds.

Beadnell: East of the harbour are the remains of a thirteenth-century chapel. Some think that there was an earlier chapel built by King Oswald for his sister, Ebba. It is still a lovely spot from which to view the seascape.

Alnmouth: From the shorefront a small hill is visible across the River Aln. The hill was formerly connected to the village of Alnmouth but cut off when the river changed its course in a massive storm. The hill is thought to be the site of the Synod of Twyford, at which Cuthbert was elected bishop. Also visible, but not visitable, is Coquet Island, now a significant bird sanctuary. In the seventh century it was the site of an Anglo-Saxon monastery. Abbess Aelfflaed of Whitby met here with Cuthbert to discuss the fate of her brother, King Ecgfrith, and to raise the question of Cuthbert accepting a bishopric.

Day 2

Hexham and Heavenfield: *The Power and the Glory*

It may seem odd to include a battlefield in a list of holy places, but the site at Heavenfield is very significant, for it was the place where the Christian king Oswald defeated the joint armies of the pagan king Penda and the Christian Cadwalla in 634. Following the battle Oswald introduced into his kingdom Irish missionaries under the leadership of Aidan (see Day 1). Today it is an isolated place, with extensive views and a strong sense of peace.

The nearby town of Hexham is built around its ancient abbey, one of the oldest and most remarkable churches in the country. It was here that Bishop Wilfrid founded a monastery and built a church in the style he had seen in Rome itself. The crypt under the church dates back to the seventh century and was designed by Wilfrid to display holy relics to pilgrims.

The holy people are perhaps less straightforward than Aidan, Cuthbert and Eadfrith from Day 1: Oswald was a warrior king, and the complex Bishop Wilfrid was hated by many people in his own day; however, it is important to read about their lives before making a judgment. I have also included Wilfrid's less well-known successor, Bishop Acca, who was known as a holy man and was a good friend both to Wilfrid and to Bede.

PEOPLE

Oswald (605–42)

Oswald makes an unusual holy person: he was best known for his fighting abilities and, though killed in battle against a pagan king, was not originally regarded as a martyr. To understand why he was and might still be considered holy we need to hear his story.

Oswald was born around 605 into the royal family of Bernicia, the northern half of Northumbria, with its main base at Bamburgh. His father was Ethelfrith, a powerful king who added Deira (roughly modern Yorkshire) to his kingdom, defeated the Scots in 603 and soon after that defeated an army of British Christians near Chester. Oswald was the middle of three sons (Eanfrith, Oswald and Oswy). They were raised as warriors in the pagan tradition of the Angles, but their lives were changed forever in 616, when their father was killed in battle against his brother-in-law Edwin of Deira. The children fled to Scotland – the young Oswald, aged eleven, and Oswy, aged four, going to Iona – because of its reputation for learning and the protection it offered. Seventeen years of exile followed, during which Oswald learned both warcraft and Christianity. Oswald probably fought with his Irish hosts in Ireland, and he was baptized into the Christian faith on Iona. Commitment to Christianity was not just a religious decision but had political overtones too: his father's gods had ultimately failed him, whilst Oswald was surrounded by examples of successful Christian kings.

After Edwin's death in 633 Ethelfrith's eldest son Eanfrith took the opportunity to seize back power for his family, but he was in turn killed by the forces of Cadwalla and Penda. Thus Oswald came to avenge his brother's death and took his army as far south as Hadrian's Wall. Bede tells of how Oswald set up a sign of the cross and prayed for God's help in the forthcoming battle. The larger army of Cadwalla was defeated in the battle of Heavenfield and Cadwalla himself was killed.

Oswald was determined to see his subjects won to the Christian faith. For missionaries he turned to Iona, rather than the Roman centre of Kent, which had been responsible for the first missionaries under Paulinus. After a false start, Aidan was sent and he worked closely with Oswald, who even acted as his interpreter at times. Oswald gave Aidan Lindisfarne as his centre and their cooperation resulted in the establishing of the church in the region.

Oswald was known to Bede as a great warrior king, but Bede preferred to emphasize his generosity to the poor. We heard the story of an Easter feast with Aidan (see Day 1). They were about to bless the food when a servant informed the king of a great crowd of needy people sitting outside. The king ordered his own food to be taken out and the silver dish on which it had been served to be broken up and distributed amongst them.

In fact Oswald was successful in gaining power over many other people – British, Pictish, Scottish and English – and he is unique in Bede's account as a saint king. For he is presented not as a martyr, but as a king who ruled as a Christian, a demanding calling at any time, and certainly in an era when power was kept through force and when it was necessary to reward your own warrior elite. His death came in battle against the pagan Penda of Mercia, near Oswestry, in 642. His head was cut off and displayed, but regained by his brother Oswy and kept as a relic. It eventually found its way into Cuthbert's coffin and is believed to still be in the shrine at Durham Cathedral (see Day 5).

In remembering his life we will probably be aware of the ambiguity of celebrating a warrior king, who could only bring about the conversion of his people through his success in battle. Yet we must also remember the circumstances of his time, when fighting between tribes was commonplace and Christianity had to compete with other religions. Oswald does seem to have shown elements of compassion alongside his fighting qualities, and his friendship with the gentle Aidan speaks for itself. We can celebrate his apparent desire to seek a better way to rule his people, a practical form of holiness.

Wilfrid (634–709)

Wilfrid is not always regarded as a holy person in our day, for he is now mostly remembered for his part in the supposed battle between a bureaucratic and remote Roman church, and a spiritually sensitive Celtic church. There is a myth that suggests that Wilfrid damaged the church at the Synod of Whitby by destroying the truer, spiritually alive faction and so the church has never been the same since. This is not a fair picture either of the synod (see Day 7) or of Wilfrid himself, for he was a complex character who inspired great affection in his followers, as well as opposition amongst many other people.

We know quite a lot about Wilfrid from Bede's *Ecclesiastical History* and also from a second source, which gives a different picture, written by Wilfrid's follower, Eddius Stephanus (Stephen). Stephen was a priest at Wilfrid's monastery of Ripon and wrote the *Life of Wilfrid* within six years of his death, fifteen years before Bede's work. It is full of rich detail, though Stephen is also very partisan in presenting Wilfrid as always right and his opponents as always wrong. This is hagiography at its most extreme!

Wilfrid, the son of an Anglo-Saxon noble, was born in 634, within a year or so of Cuthbert, though he lived a quarter of a century longer. In 648, at the age of fourteen, he joined the Northumbrian court of Oswy and found favour with the queen, Eanfled. However, he was keen to train as a monk, and not long after, he entered the monastery on Holy Island, still under the leadership of Bishop Aidan. This was the year that Hilda came back to Northumbria and started a community at the mouth of the River Wear. Bede noted his obedience and humility. He was quick to learn the Psalter and then the Gospels, and he was marked out as a man with a future. However, it may be that the death of Aidan three years later unsettled him; soon afterwards he wanted to visit Rome.

The journey to Rome was a long one, involving a long wait in Canterbury on the way, until Biscop Baducing (see Day 3) arrived and the young Wilfrid could join his travelling party. For Wilfrid there was the best part of another year in Lyon, an important commercial and political centre. Archbishop Annemundus of Lyon took to Wilfrid and offered him a governorship, and marriage to his niece, and he was still not twenty!

In Rome he was instructed for a year by Archdeacon Boniface in Scripture and Canon law, including the correct way to calculate the date of Easter. Before leaving Rome Wilfrid met Pope Eugene for a blessing and set off with relics, textiles, church plate and gemstones.

On the return journey he spent three crucial years in Lyon, where Archbishop Annemundus groomed him as a possible successor in the church. Wilfrid received the monastic tonsure at the hand of the archbishop – the Roman tonsure of course. In Annemundus he saw how a bishop might work closely with the secular ruler (the local count was his brother), but then so had Aidan with Oswald. What was different was the sense that a church leader in this context was a social equal of the secular leaders, a public servant in the ancient tradition of the Roman empire. Public magnificence was combined (generally) with private austerity. As aristocrats with means they could rebuke kings, distribute wealth and provide education.

The archbishop was martyred at the instigation of the local ruler, who feared the growing influence of the church. Wilfrid was willing to die with the archbishop, but as a foreigner with connections he was spared to be sent back to his homeland. This traumatic experience seems to have reinforced the sense in Wilfrid that this way of leading the church and the Continental practices of Gaul were correct; this also implied that some of the practices he had learned on Holy Island were not.

This time away from Northumbria was absolutely crucial for Wilfrid's development: a year in Canterbury, a year in Lyon, a year in Rome and a further three years in Lyon. These were major centres of Christianity, with excellent written records and up-to-date liturgical practices. Cuthbert never travelled out of Northumbria and so did not encounter the force of other versions of Christianity first hand in the same way as Wilfrid.

Once back in Northumbria, he was active in promoting the reformed customs of worship that he had learned in Rome and Lyon. He was intelligent and well connected through his travels and his links to the royal family, and he became firm friends with Alchfrid, son of Oswy and Eanfled. Within a couple of years of his return Alchfrid gave Wilfrid the monastery at Ripon, effectively evicting the group from Melrose, which had included Cuthbert. Wilfrid became the Abbot of Ripon in 661, still only twenty-seven, and he was ordained priest by Bishop Agilbert of Dorchester two years later.

Wilfrid was a key speaker at the Synod of Whitby (see Appendix), and though he won the arguments he did not win many friends. Bishop Colman chose to leave Lindisfarne after the synod, and a new bishop was needed; Oswy chose Tuda, and then Chad. Oswy's son Alchfrid decided to send Wilfrid to Gaul for consecration.

But he was gone too long, for by the time Wilfrid returned Chad was well established as bishop, and Wilfrid's patron Alchfrid had rebelled against his father and was killed. Wilfrid retired to his monastery at Ripon, until a new Archbishop of Canterbury, Theodore, moved Chad to Mercia and appointed Wilfrid as Bishop of York. Over the next ten years Wilfrid was very successful, and Ripon and Hexham were built up as major Christian centres.

Wilfrid's churches at Ripon and Hexham were constructed in the 660s and 670s. Apart from a cathedral church in York, built in the 620s, they were, as far as we know, the first stone buildings erected in Northumbria since the Roman legions left Britain in 410. For the Anglo-Saxons, used to single-storey timber and thatch houses, they must have seemed awesomely grand and permanent.

In our own day we tend to be romantic about simpler buildings, and the first churches of Aidan and his followers were built of wood. But there are important lessons in the transformation from wood to stone – lessons that may round out and challenge our sense of holiness:

• The solid stone is a physical reminder of the majesty of God, crucial in an age in which ordinary folk needed stability.

• We are called to belong to a spiritual temple in which Christ is the cornerstone, the foundation of our life together as a Christian community.

• The permanence of stone churches teaches us the value of a continuing community, able to represent the faithfulness of God.

• A further important aspect of a continuing community lies in its ability to promote learning, especially in valuing the word of God, recorded in handwritten Gospels of the highest quality.

Sadly Wilfrid had the knack of making enemies as well as friends, and he was banished from his bishopric – no fewer than three times. Unlike his colleagues Wilfrid does not seem to have been flexible with the vagaries of the kings; he was either principled or stubborn, depending on your point of view.

Oswy's son Ecgfrith was now ruler of Northumbria, but Wilfrid fell out with him by supporting his queen, Ethelthryth, who wished to remain a virgin and to enter a monastery. Wilfrid was motivated by religious aims, but he was also in danger of becoming a rival to the king, as his monasteries accumulated land and gifts, following the Gaulish pattern of independence from the king.

As a result of his travels he became a successful missionary bishop in Frisia (Holland) and amongst the pagan Anglo-Saxons in Sussex and the Isle of Wight, perhaps a legacy of Aidan's influence. In his late forties, at a time when many were reaching the end of their days, he found himself in Sussex, then a pagan and godless place, and began to preach the good news of salvation. Bede recounts that the people were suffering a dreadful famine and that Wilfrid taught them how to fish in the sea. After some months of this people's hearts were opened, and many were baptized.

After final, though partial, vindication by the Pope in 705 he was made Bishop of Hexham, and after many years of dispute the monasteries of Ripon and Hexham were restored to him. He died in 709 at one of his monasteries at Oundle, and was taken back for burial at his favourite site of Ripon.

Wilfrid's example of holiness is not popular today and was controversial in his own time. But he clearly did have loyal followers who recognized his personal commitment to Christ and knew that his own lifestyle was austere. This often makes people uncomfortable, because he was also committed to seeking power and influence for the church. Wilfrid's life poses difficult questions about whether holiness should only be a matter of private lifestyle or whether it should also include the ways we organize our society.

Acca (died 737 or 740)

Acca became Bishop of Hexham in 709 after the death of Wilfrid. He was a close friend of both Wilfrid and Bede, and was much loved in Hexham. His holiness was not of the heroic kind, but a gentler, more encouraging version. He had been trained early on in the household of Bishop Bosa of York, himself a monk from Whitby. Later he joined Wilfrid, who became his mentor; he was a loyal priest, and he eventually accompanied him on his last journey to Rome.

Acca devoted his life to building up the faith in Northumbria, developing Hexham as a centre of learning and devotion. Bede knew him personally and described him as 'a man of great energy and noble in the sight of God and man'. He added many relics to the church and built side-chapels for them; he collected books and manuscripts for the library; he found sacred vessels to enhance the church; and he brought a famous singer, Maban, from Canterbury to teach Gregorian chant. Acca himself was both a first-class singer and learned in the Bible.

His later years are shrouded in mystery: he was deposed around 732, perhaps for political reasons. It is not clear when he died – both 737 and 740 are recorded in different sources – but his remains were brought back to Hexham. The cross believed to have marked his grave is now reconstructed in the south transept of the abbey, in a prominent place close to the entry door.

Acca is a reminder that holiness can mean steady work in God's service, helping others in their faith and supporting the work of better-known people. For every Wilfrid or Cuthbert there are many people who quietly live out their faith and show to the people around them the reality of the God they trust in.

PLACES

Heavenfield

Heading south from Holy Island there is beautiful and wild countryside, and small settlements are scattered about, many of which are on sites that were known to Aidan and Cuthbert. Eventually the ridges that carry Hadrian's Wall come into view; it was on the wall that a crucial battle was fought in 634 at Heavenfield. The kingdom of Northumbria was held briefly by Cadwalla, a British leader, but Oswald of the old northern ruling family of Bernicia had gathered his army to meet the British army advancing up the Roman Dere Street.

Bede wrote of Cadwalla's 'savage tyranny' and was delighted that Oswald's army defeated him there. The site of the battle is now marked by the chapel of St Oswald, built in 1737 to replace the earlier structures. The first chapel was built in the late seventh century by the monks of Hexham to celebrate Oswald's victory; a pilgrimage from Hexham to Heavenfield is still held on the first Saturday in August for St Oswald's Day (5 August). A modern cross standing in the adjoining lay-by is a useful landmark.

Visitors can take time to meditate in the simple chapel and also to look over the expanses of Northumbria. The scene stretches far to the north across the land regained by Oswald, and on the clearest days the Cheviot summit is visible, inland from Holy Island. The violence of the battle seems far away in this peaceful setting. The contrast between the bloody history of this site and the serenity it offers visitors today might challenge our very ideas of what makes a place 'holy'.

Hexham Abbey

There has been a church here for over 1,300 years, since Queen Etheldreda of York granted the land to Wilfrid, Bishop of York, in the 670s. He built a Benedictine abbey in the style he had learned in Rome and Gaul, and he sent for builders from Europe who could reintroduce the lost art of cement making. Wilfrid's church was a fine one, with crypts, towering columns creating side aisles, high walls and spiral staircases. His somewhat ingratiating biographer was clearly impressed, for he wrote, 'We have never heard of its like this side of the Alps' (*Life of Wilfrid*, Chapter 22). A panel on the right of the entrance sets Hexham in the context of other Anglo-Saxon churches in Northumbria, including Lindisfarne, Monkwearmouth and Whitby.

Only the Saxon crypt still remains from Wilfrid's church, but it is worth visiting for this alone, for the rooms and passages are intact from the seventh century. Wilfrid had gained inspiration from the churches he had seen in Rome and wanted to create a setting to inspire his own people. The steep descent takes one into the world of the first pilgrims, who came to get a glimpse of the cloth sanctified by the relics said to come from St Andrew. They would inch their way through in the gloom until they reached the antechamber, from where they could see into the smoky central chamber with its walls painted with biblical scenes and the holy casket placed directly below the high altar.

In the crypt, as in the rest of the church, the builders reused worked stone from the Roman wall and the fort at Corbridge. Inscriptions can be seen on many stones, indicating that they have been reused in this way over the centuries, through all the phases of rebuilding. The use of stones from a pre-Christian era may speak to us of the manner in which God is able to take all our experience and use it to his glory, though we may need to allow the master builder to reshape us.

This is a place in which Christian prayer has been offered for many centuries, and the many changes in the building reflect the changing beliefs of the people. This can be seen in the importance of the relics in the early medieval period; the grand rebuilding in the late medieval period, revealing a powerful God; the simplification of the Reformation; and, more recently, the rediscovery of the value of symbolism. Should you have the opportunity to visit, take time to explore the many riches of this building and ask yourself how it speaks to you of God. There are several places set aside for personal prayer, including the chapel of St Wilfrid at the east end.

Prayer
Gracious God,

You build the church from Jesus the living stone
and accepted the varied and imperfect gifts of Oswald and Wilfrid
*   and Acca.*

Take the rough stones of our lives
and use and reuse them as part of your living temple,
that we may offer our own spiritual sacrifice through Jesus Christ.

Practicalities

St Oswald, Heavenfield

The site of the battle of Heavenfield is marked by the chapel of St Oswald. It is reached across a field from the B6318 road (OS ref 936694), about a mile east of the crossing of the River North Tyne at Chollerford. There is some parking in a lay-by on the north side of the road.

St Oswald's Tearoom is ¼ mile east of the chapel, and serves Fairtrade drinks and home-made cakes. Open 10 a.m.–4.30 p.m., Friday, Saturday and Sunday in March, April and November; Tuesday to Sunday and Bank Holidays from May to October. *http://www.britannia.com/tours/batnorthumb/heavenfield.html*

Hexham Abbey

From Heavenfield the journey to Hexham is easy. Follow the line of the wall west to the A6079 and turn left (south) and go down the attractive valley of the River North Tyne, following signs into Hexham and the abbey.

Hexham is an ancient market town just south of the A69. The abbey is well signed from the main road. Parking is on the edge of the town centre. Park close to the Tourist Information Centre, and to its right there is pedestrian access to the marketplace and the abbey.

The crypt can be visited each day at 11 a.m. and 3.30 p.m. by asking the verger or steward on duty.

Teas are served in the Monastic Workshop each Tuesday, Saturday and Sunday from 1.30 p.m. to 5 p.m., June to September. There are plenty of cafés in the town at other times. *http://www.hexhamabbey.org.uk/*

Other places

Corbridge: Three miles east of Hexham is the attractive market town of Corbridge. The church of St Andrew was founded in the seventh century, and Saxon features can be seen in the base of the tower and the baptistery. Next to the church is a most unusual medieval vicarage, the Vicar's Pele, with its castle-like features to protect the vicar from the Scots.

Hadrian's Wall: The wall is easily accessible from Hexham; information is available at the Tourist Information Centre. *http://www.hadrians-wall.org/*

Tynemouth Priory: The priory lies on the north bank of the Tyne on the site of a seventh-century monastery, the burial place of Oswin, sainted King of Northumbria. The Benedictine priory was re-founded around 1090, though now only the east end survives to full height. It offers a wonderful view over the estuary.

http://www.english-heritage.org.uk/server/show/nav.13480

Jarrow and Monkwearmouth:
The Bede Connection

Jarrow and Monkwearmouth are important places in the history of England, for it was here that Bede, the first historian of England, lived and wrote. That would be enough to make these places worth visiting, but there is more. There are extensive remains of buildings dating back to Bede's time; St Peter's Monkwearmouth is one of the oldest churches in England and is still in regular use. At Jarrow an atmospheric church lies amidst the ruins of a medieval monastery, and nearby is Bede's World, an excellent modern museum, complete with an Anglo-Saxon village. There is another side to Monkwearmouth: it is the birthplace of the modern Pentecostal Movement in the UK, and following celebrations of its centenary in 2007 increasing attention has been given to this more recent history and a new form of pilgrimage.

The holy people for this Day include: Bede the monk, historian, Bible scholar and scientist; Bede's first mentor, Benedict Biscop, who founded the monastery of Wearmouth-Jarrow; Bede's second mentor, the faithful abbot Ceolfrith; and Alexander and Mary Boddy, a vicar of the Church of England and his wife, who were also the first leaders of the Pentecostal Movement, with ministries that took them throughout the UK, and also to Europe and North America.

People

Bede (673–735)

Aidan, Hilda and Cuthbert all show the strong influence of the Irish church, via Iona and Lindisfarne. But Bede was brought up and formed by the Roman pattern. Though he sought to be fair to the Irish version of Christianity, and admired Aidan, he regarded their way as not quite right. His own holiness was not that of the activist, but was based on the Benedictine pattern of monastic prayer, seven times a day, and on his formidable scholarship.

Bede was born around 673, within the lifetime of Cuthbert, and less than forty years after the start of Aidan's mission. We know a little about his life from his own writing, especially his note at the end of his *Ecclesiastical History of the English People*.

He was born in the area of what became monastic land owned by Wearmouth, and a year or so later Benedict Biscop founded the monastery there. When Bede was aged seven, around 680, he was entered into the monastery at Wearmouth by his kinsfolk. We don't know why: perhaps he had been orphaned, or perhaps they realized he was very able intellectually and thought a monastic education would be good for him. He himself delighted in becoming a monk and later a priest.

A year later the sister monastery at Jarrow was founded, and Abbot Ceolfrith probably took the boy Bede, along with about twenty monks. In 686 a terrible plague reduced the monastery to the abbot and a boy. The boy is almost certainly Bede himself, aged thirteen. This dreadful experience developed his affection for Ceolfrith. We know that he 'took delight in learning, teaching, and writing' and his ability was great, for he was ordained deacon in his nineteenth year, six years younger than the usual minimum age. It was permitted to ordain younger men in cases of outstanding learning and piety, but as much as six years early indicates the high regard in which Ceolfrith held him.

The rest of his life was spent as a scholar monk – joining in the daily round of prayer, preaching and presiding at the Eucharist – and in manual work as well as study. We know he visited Lindisfarne once to discuss the life of Cuthbert that he was writing; he went to another, unnamed monastery to discuss issues in chronology with a fellow priest; and he went to York towards the end of his life. Otherwise he seems to have been content to stay within his monastery, and to travel in his mind, using the great library built up by Biscop and Ceolfrith.

His most famous work today is his *Ecclesiastical History*. Within a few years of its completion in 731 it was being requested throughout England and soon Continental Europe. One hundred years later Alfred had it translated into English as one of the books 'most necessary for all men to know'. Without it we would not know of Hilda and Caedmon, Chad and Cedd, Oswald and Edwin. There is no comparable history in any other part of Europe at that period; it was the first time anyone had tried to set down the spiritual history of his people.

In organizing the material that he had collected over many years he decided to use the system of *Anno Domini* dating, instead of using the years of the various rulers, problematic with so many kingdoms in existence at once. The AD system had been devised two centuries earlier, but Bede was the most important writer in popularizing its use.

Bede also wrote several books on saints, of which the most important to us are his *Lives of the Abbots of Wearmouth/Jarrow* and his poetic and prose *Lives of Cuthbert*. His writings also included works about the natural world. His knowledge was vast: he knew that the earth was a sphere; he knew about the annual movement of the sun into the north and south hemispheres from the evidence of varying lengths of shadows; he knew that the moon influenced the cycle of the tides. He wrote on calculating time and the date of Easter.

Bishop Boniface, the Anglo-Saxon missionary to Germany, wrote that Bede 'shone forth as a lantern in the church by his scriptural commentary', and his fifty-five commentaries on books of the Bible were widely circulated. Bede himself saw this as his most important work. He was committed to teaching the Bible in his native Anglo-Saxon, even though he was a fine scholar in Latin and Greek, and knew some Hebrew. Long before Luther or Tyndale or Wycliffe, Bede knew that most people would not learn these languages and needed the Scriptures to be read in their own tongue. His commentaries were soon being copied by the Scriptorium at Wearmouth and being sent all over Europe. Because of his biblical scholarship Bede was eventually called a Doctor of the Church by Pope Leo XIII in 1899 – the only Englishman to be given this honour.

His amazing output was made possible by the extensive library in his monastery, but it was not just the library that was important. Other people were too. Time and again we find Bede referring to people who had told him their stories. In his *Ecclesiastical History*, he recounts some disturbing events in the monastery of Coldingham in the 680s and carefully explains that his informant was a fellow priest, Edgils, who, having lived in that monastery at the time, was an eyewitness. This man then came to live in Bede's monastery. In his prose *Life of Cuthbert* he includes a lengthy quotation about the saint's death from Herefrith, a priest and then abbot of Lindisfarne. He had been Cuthbert's personal attendant during his final illness and so could give a graphic account of his last days.

Bede took opportunities to discuss scholarly issues with others whenever possible. He had a long friendship with Bishop

Acca of Hexham (see Day 2). He sent him draft commentaries for comment, whilst later Acca persuaded him to write a commentary on Acts. Yet another source was the London priest Nothhelm, later Archbishop of Canterbury; he spoke personally with Bede about the mission of the church in Kent and London.

Bede's death in 735 was described in a letter by one of his pupils. He fell ill before Easter, but continued to pray and to chant the Psalter, despite his breathlessness. Even on his last day he was translating his beloved Gospel of John into Anglo-Saxon. Here was the heart of Bede's mission: to make the gospel accessible to his own English people. (Sadly this translation of John's Gospel has not come down to us.) He was buried in Jarrow, but his reputation was so great that after the founding of Durham Cathedral a priest from Durham stole his bones to add to their collection. There they remain to this day, at the west end in the Galilee Chapel (see Day 5).

His holiness was a disciplined matter, devoted and faithful: faithful to God in prayer, faithful to his community in serving, faithful to truth in his scholarship. Bede's life challenges us to consider where we are called to be faithful in our own lives and to think about where we draw strength from to continue our devotion.

Benedict Biscop (628–89)

Like all the major church leaders we know from the seventh century, Biscop was of high social status – 'noble birth' in Bede's language – one of King Oswy's thanes, a military rank below an earl. However, at the age of twenty-five he put aside this status to pursue the religious life. We don't know what prompted him in this new life, but eventually he added the name Benedict to his own, a sign that he wanted to take seriously the monastic life shaped by the Rule of St Benedict.

Here is a man whose desire to be holy took him away from the court and military concerns into a life of prayer. He first visited Rome as a pilgrim, travelling with Wilfrid as far as Lyon, and he brought back ideas on how the church should develop. After a second visit he was admitted as a monk at Lerins, an island off Cannes, and after two years' training he visited Rome for a third time. During his time there he was ordered by the Pope to accompany the new Archbishop of Canterbury, Theodore, as guide and interpreter. This led to his appointment as Abbot of St Peter's monastery in Canterbury.

Just two years later, around 671, he set off on a fourth journey to Rome, this time collecting many books on a wide range of topics and also relics of apostles and saints. He found himself in 674 back in his native Northumbria, able to speak with King Ecgfrith, son of Oswy, about his vision for developing the monastic life. As mentioned below in the section on St Peter's Church he was given seventy hides of land, and the new monastery in Wearmouth was quickly begun in the Gaulish style.

The new monastery clearly flourished under his wise leadership, and after five years Biscop went on a fifth journey to Rome, taking Ceolfrith with him this time, with the aim of enhancing the monastery in Wearmouth. Bede lists five spiritual treasures that Biscop brought back with him from Rome to assist the spiritual growth of the monks. First were the numerous additional books. Second were many more relics, which were later shared with other churches. Third was the introduction of singing psalms and the whole service according to the Roman pattern. He was able to bring back John, the chief cantor (singer) from St Peter's Rome, to teach this to the monks and to record the teaching in writing. The fourth treasure was a legal document from the Pope guaranteeing the monastery's independence, a separation of church and state only possible with the king's approval. Finally, for the decoration of the church there were holy pictures of Mary and the twelve apostles, Gospel scenes and the Last Judgment; here was the Christian message spelled out in pictures for all to see.

Bede saw this to be a very important legacy, and in a homily about Biscop he wrote:

'He worked so zealously that we are freed from the need to labour in this way; he journeyed so many times to places across the sea, that we, abounding in all the resources of spiritual knowledge, can as a result be at peace within the cloisters of the monastery, with secure freedom to serve Christ.' (Homilies *Book 1, no.13 in Benedicta Ward,* The Venerable Bede)

With the support of Ecgfrith, he founded St Paul's Jarrow in 681. To share the burden of leadership Biscop appointed Ceolfrith to rule in Jarrow and Eosterwine in Wearmouth. This gave him the opportunity for a final visit to Rome, bringing back many more books and pictures, this time on the life of Jesus and on Old Testament themes.

His return was marked by sadness, for the plague had killed Eosterwine and many other monks in both Wearmouth and Jarrow. Biscop's own death came after three years of creeping paralysis, spreading from his lower limbs. Bede records two concerns of the dying Biscop: the maintenance of the extensive library in one place, and the election of a new abbot from amongst their own number (according to the Rule of Benedict) and not a member of his family (as often happened in Irish and Germanic monasteries). The appointment of Ceolfrith over the 'one monastery in two places' was agreed before Biscop's death. He was buried near the altar in St Peter's Monkwearmouth.

Biscop illustrates holiness in both prayer and action, in settled community and on the move. In his case they appear to be unified by the desire to build a new family in Christ, held together by monastic discipline and able to demonstrate the gospel in an unstable society. Despite his journeying he remained committed to living out the gospel amongst his own people, and he used his gifts of leadership and influence to that end.

Ceolfrith (642–716)

Ceolfrith is a less well-known figure from the seventh century, but a key person in ensuring that Biscop's vision was established during Biscop's lifetime and after his death. Ceolfrith too was of noble birth, with Christian parents noted for their generosity. He joined a monastery at the age of eighteen, following the example of his elder brother. Later he studied at Ripon under Wilfrid, and he was ordained priest by Wilfrid at the age of twenty-seven (669), before further study in Kent and East Anglia. Returning to Northumbria he was well equipped to support Biscop in the foundation of Wearmouth in 674 and he was made prior, the second-in-charge. He accompanied Biscop in travelling to Rome in 680, and on their return the following year he took charge of the new monastery at Jarrow.

His wisdom and leadership were evident in the trust that Biscop placed in him, but these were put to the test when so many monks of the community died in the plague of 685. He then had to find new monks and take in existing monks from elsewhere, a demanding task of creating and training a new community. As Biscop came to the end of his life Ceolfrith became abbot of the 'one monastery in two places', and he ruled the community for a further twenty-seven years. During this long period he was noted for his desire for God's justice, correcting wrongdoers, and also for encouraging those who were repentant. He was said to be generous in giving to the poor and faithful in his prayer life. These might seem like no more than conventional praises of a monk and abbot, but we know that other men in such positions were not praised in this way, and we can take seriously Ceolfrith's own practical holiness, caring for those in need.

Ceolfrith continued the development of the Wearmouth-Jarrow library; it was truly one of the great libraries of Western Christendom in the eighth century. The Scriptorium was kept very busy, producing copies of the works they held, of Bede's own works and, most importantly, of the Scriptures. In Ceolfrith's time some three copies of the Scriptures were made, of which one – the Codex Amiatinus – remains. It is now in a library in Florence, though recently facsimiles have been made and brought to Sunderland. This book contains a massive 1,029 folio sheets – four times the 259 folios in the Lindisfarne Gospels! Most of these pages had to come from a different animal hide, so the investment of resources is enormous. The text itself in the codex is the best and earliest copy we have of Jerome's Latin translation, often known as the Vulgate, so it is of huge significance in the history of the translation of the Bible.

By 716 Ceolfrith was in his seventies and had been abbot for longer than many people lived at that time. Coming to the end of his long life he wanted to end his days in Rome, and he secretly made preparations to do so. After a sad departure, deeply moving for Bede and others who had known him for so long, he set off with eighty companions, leaving behind a monastic community now over 600 strong. They took with them many gifts, the most important being the great copy of the Bible, the Codex Amiatinus, for the Pope. Sadly the journey was too much for Ceolfrith and he died at Langres in Burgundy. He was buried in the local monastery, though later his body was returned to Jarrow. The party split three ways, one group returning home with sad news, one group staying with the body and the third continuing to Rome with their gifts.

Ceolfrith was revered in his own lifetime as a man of generosity, good judgment and devotion to God, qualities that took root in his Christian upbringing and were cultivated by his monastic training. His long and fruitful life serves as an encouragement to our own faithfulness in the small things as well as the large.

Alexander Boddy (1854–1930) and Mary Boddy (1855–1928)

It may seem odd to include two much more recent characters in this collection of holy people, but Alexander and Mary Boddy deserve to be better known for their long Christian service in Monkwearmouth. They were conscious of living so close to the historic centre of Wearmouth, and Alexander studied Bede's work in his ordination training. Their most obvious public contribution was in establishing the Pentecostal Movement in the UK, but they also served for many years amongst the industrial workers of the busiest shipbuilding port in the world.

Both their fathers were vicars, though Alexander was brought up in one of the poorest parts of the rapidly expanding town of Manchester, whereas Mary was brought up in the countryside. Her health suffered badly when, after marrying Alexander, the couple moved into the vicarage between an ironworks and a rope works. Both of them were nurtured by the British version of what was called the Holiness Movement, which had origins in the teaching of John Wesley. The Keswick Convention, a week-long annual teaching convention that began in 1875 and still continues, took up the Holiness theme. The Boddys were deeply influenced by its teaching that it was possible to overcome sin in this life by the help of God. One practical outworking of this was in Alexander's lifelong support for the Temperance

Movement, at a time when the abuse of alcohol was a serious social concern. In some ways Mary was a traditional vicar's wife, supporting her husband and concentrating on teaching women the Christian faith, but Alexander also encouraged her in public speaking, writing and prayer for individuals. Together they made a powerful team.

In their desire to know God better they held prayer meetings asking for the gift of God's Holy Spirit, and in 1907 a series of public meetings with a Methodist minister, T. B. Barratt, resulted in people having powerful spiritual experiences, including 'speaking in tongues'. This was highly controversial and attracted criticism from many in the churches and scepticism from the national newspapers. Boddy was concerned about this; in his and Mary's teaching they always emphasized the importance of love – love for God and love for neighbour. This focus on the two great commandments of Jesus was necessary in a movement that was sometimes in danger of emphasizing stirring experiences more than living out the Christian life.

Alexander and Mary had great credibility in teaching this way, for their work in the parish had long combined worship, Bible study and practical care for people. An outstanding example of their commitment occurred in 1892 in the midst of a long coal miners' strike. Other workers, including the iron workers next door, were laid off and their families quickly became destitute. Boddy collected money to run a soup kitchen for the families and even wrote to *The Times* newspaper about their predicament. He raised over £500, and the grateful families later presented him with a silver communion set and Mary with a silver tea urn.

Their hard work in Monkwearmouth was very wearing, and late in life the Bishop of Durham moved them to the country parish of Pittington, just east of Durham (see Day 4). They continued to take their duties seriously until illness prevented them. Mary died in 1928, Alexander in 1930, and they are buried together there in the churchyard.

For the Boddys, 'Holiness' might have been a slogan, but they saw beyond the word to live out what it implied. For them it meant devotion to God in prayer and Bible study, the love of people in need and the sharing of the good gifts they had found in God through the Holy Spirit. Their openness to God at all stages of their lives remains a challenge.

Places

St Paul's Church, Jarrow

In 681 Jarrow was settled by monks from Monkwearmouth monastery. The young Bede, aged eight, was amongst them. Like all monasteries of the time the site was chosen for its access by river, in this case the River Don, a tributary of the River Tyne. It was sheltered from the storms of the coast but at no great distance. Today it is surrounded by industrial sites, a reminder of the central part County Durham played in the nineteenth-century industrialization of Britain, and in the Jarrow March in 1936, a response to the desperate unemployment of the time.

St Paul's Church and monastery were built on land given by King Ecgfrith of Northumbria in 681. The present chancel of St Paul's Church is the original Saxon church built as a separate chapel and contains three Saxon windows, one with Saxon glass. A large basilica was built on the site of the present nave and dedicated on 23 April 685, as the dedication stone records. In 794 the Vikings raided the church and monastery, which were finally abandoned in the late ninth century. In 1074 the church was repaired and the monastery re-founded by

Prior Aldwin of Gloucestershire, becoming a daughter house of the newly formed Benedictine Community at Durham ten years later.

As the present parish church this is both a historic building and an expression of faith today. The church is well organized for casual visitors and pilgrims, for exploration and for prayer. Visitors can sit in the place in which Bede prayed, seeing some of the building he knew himself. Important features include the seventh-century foundations in the main aisle; the foot of a Saxon cross in the north nave, with its Latin inscription, 'In this unique sign, life is restored to the world'; the exhibition of Anglo-Saxon sculpture; and the dedication stone of 685, now placed above the chancel arch.

Outside are the remains of the domestic buildings, offering an insight into the practicalities of monastic living in the later medieval period. In Bede's World across the park there is an excellent exhibition of how Christianity came to north-east England, information about Bede, and a reconstruction of an Anglo-Saxon farm, complete with animals.

St Peter's Church, Monkwearmouth

The monastery Bede belonged to was described by Bede as 'one monastery in two places', with the original site being Wearmouth, or Monkwearmouth as it became known. Biscop founded the monastery in 674, on land donated by King Ecgfrith after Biscop had returned from Rome with sacred books and relics. Ecgfrith gave a generous endowment of seventy hides, notionally enough to support seventy families. This was just a couple of years after Wilfrid had begun work on Hexham and perhaps there was an element of competition, for Wilfrid also brought in masons from Gaul to build in the European manner. Biscop went one step further by bringing glaziers for the first time, and seventh-century glass can be seen in an exhibition in the church; the tradition is also celebrated in the present-day National Glass Centre.

Some parts of the original church have survived – the west wall of the present nave and the lowest stage of the tower. The west porch was probably built shortly afterwards, and the open arch at the porch entrance, decorated with carvings of beaked, reptile-like creatures, dates from the late seventh or early eighth centuries. There is little doubt that Bede himself would have seen these carvings and walked through the archway. The doorway is reputed to be the oldest in Europe still in its original place and with its original design. The remainder of the tower, above the porch, was constructed later; the difference in building styles can be clearly seen.

Inside the building are fine modern stained glass windows, commemorating the people associated with the monastery, five at the east end and three more in the north aisle. There is an excellent exhibition of the history of the church, including its long association with John Wesley, who preached here regularly on his visits to Sunderland.

All Saints' Church and Parish Hall, Monkwearmouth

This was the first parish in the Church of England to hold Pentecostal meetings, in which prayer for 'baptism in the Spirit' was offered. Most of the meetings were held in the Parish Hall in Fulwell Road but some took place in the church itself. The parish of All Saints, Monkwearmouth, had been formed out of that of St Peter's, Monkwearmouth, in 1844. The first vicar was unable to cope with the work required in an urbanizing parish, where both population and industry were rapidly increasing, and by the 1870s he had acquired a reputation for drunkenness. What had been a new church building was in a bad way by the

time Alexander Boddy became vicar in 1886, but he began to put things right. The building today is well cared for, and in the small hall there are mementoes of previous vicars and especially the work of Boddy. Stained-glass windows depict appropriate biblical passages in memory of the Boddys: for Mary there is a pair of windows, picturing the Mary who sat at the feet of Jesus listening to his words; for Alexander, the Good Shepherd carrying a lamb, a fitting image for a man who devoted his life as shepherd to his parish and to Pentecostal people around the world.

The Parish Hall down the road has a stone that states, 'When the fire fell it burned up the debt', dated September 1907. This is a reference to the impact of the spiritual outpouring in September 1907: people were so deeply affected that they were ready to give generously in order to support the work Boddy had started. The hall was taken over by a Pentecostal church in 1996, which added another stone, stating, 'When the fire fell again there was no debt', recording their story of faith and provision for their needs.

Prayer

Holy Spirit of God,
You inspired Bede with gifts of learning and wisdom.

Holy Spirit of God,
You inspired Biscop with gifts of vision and energy.

Holy Spirit of God,
You inspired Ceolfrith with gifts of generosity and faithfulness.

Holy Spirit of God,
You inspired the Boddys with gifts of love and openness.

Holy Spirit of God,
Open us to your gifts today

… of learning and wisdom

… of vision and energy

… of generosity and faithfulness

… of love and openness.

Holy Spirit of God,
Come to us, we pray.

Practicalities

St Paul's Church, Jarrow

From Hexham the easiest route by car to Jarrow is to take the A69 towards Newcastle as far as the A1. Go south on the A1 over the Tyne as far as signs for Sunderland via the A1231 and the A194(M). Take the A194(M) and the A194 until it meets the A19 and turn north. Bede's World at Jarrow is signed from the A19, just before the Tyne tunnel. There is car parking on the road by St Paul's Church or nearby at Bede's World. The church

is usually open from Monday to Saturday, 10 a.m.–4 p.m. and
Sunday, 2.30 p.m.–4 p.m.
http://www.jarrowparish.info/stpauls.html
Meals and drinks are available at Jarrow Hall café every day.
http://www.bedesworld.co.uk/shopcafe-cafe.php

Pilgrims on foot could use the Hadrian's Wall path from
Heavenfield as far as Wallsend (30 miles), and then catch a bus
to Jarrow.
http://www.nationaltrail.co.uk/hadrianswall/

Bede's World, Jarrow

Follow the instructions above to find this excellent exhibition
on Bede and the Anglo-Saxon church. There is a demonstration
Anglo-Saxon farm, complete with animals and crops.
http://www.bedesworld.co.uk/

St Peter's Church, Monkwearmouth

To reach Monkwearmouth, a district of Sunderland, head back
to the A19 and travel south to the A184. Turn left towards
Boldon and follow the road into Sunderland. Follow signs for
the National Glass Centre; there are signs to St Peter's Church
as you get close to the Glass Centre. There is parking on the
road by the church or at the Glass Centre. (From the Glass
Centre, walk to the right of the university buildings, up a short
flight of steps, and walk left round the churchyard perimeter
fence to the entrance. This is the site of the original monastic
buildings.)

The church is open weekdays from 2 p.m. to 4.30 p.m. and
many mornings. Check with the Parish Office on 0191 516 0135.

All Saints' Church, Monkwearmouth

All Saints' Church, associated with Alexander Boddy, is a ten-minute walk from St Peter's Church on Fulwell Road, and a drive round the one-way system. The former parish hall is a short walk down Fulwell Road, past The Cambridge pub. All Saints is open by arrangement with the Parish Office on 0191 516 0135.

There is now a good walking route between Jarrow and Monkwearmouth on the 12-mile Bede's Way.
http://www.wearmouth-jarrow.org.uk/index.php?pageId=20

From Sunderland to Durham: *Hidden Stories*

This Day offers the opportunity to explore some stories and places of great interest, though perhaps less well known than others in this guide. We learn about the reformer Bernard Gilpin (Houghton-le-Spring); the church at Pittington, with its amazing twelfth-century wall paintings, architecture related to the cathedral and the final parish of Boddy; the ancient resting place of Cuthbert at Chester-le-Street; and the beautiful Finchale Priory, the home of the eccentric monk Godric.

PEOPLE

Bernard Gilpin (1517–83/4)

Bernard Gilpin became the Archdeacon of Durham and then Rector of Houghton-le-Spring in the late 1550s and was known for his care of people in need and his passion for improving the education of his parishioners, using his large income for the benefit of others. The story of his life was written by his relative and pupil, Bishop George Carleton, and it sometimes glosses over the more negative aspects. However, we do have evidence that Gilpin was a remarkable man who made a holy impression on the people he met, whether at the king's court, the University of Oxford or in the farms of County Durham. He set himself high standards in parish ministry and helped to shape the 'middle way' encouraged by Queen Elizabeth for the Church of England.

Gilpin was born in 1517 at Kentmere Hall, Westmorland (now Cumbria), to a gentry family. He was educated at Queen's College, Oxford, in the 1530s, and studied the writings of Erasmus, one of the most important thinkers at the time of the Reformation. He received much support from Bishop Cuthbert Tunstall, who was his mother's uncle and Bishop of London from 1522 to 1530, and then Bishop of Durham from 1530 to 1559 (with some complications along the way).

Whilst Gilpin was at Oxford, he was one of the first elected students at Christ Church, the new cathedral for Oxford. He was ordained in 1541, possibly at the first ordination held there. He was clearly an able scholar, in what we might call a moderate Catholic wing of the church, joining company with Erasmus, Tunstall and Reginald Pole, later cardinal in Mary's reign. In the 1540s Gilpin was invited by Edmund Bonner, Bishop of London, to represent the more Catholic position in a series of debates in Oxford with reformers such as John Hooper, Peter Martyr and Martin Bucer. He claimed later that it was in the 1549 debate with Peter Martyr that he began to have more serious doubts about aspects of the 'Popish religion', especially over the issue of transubstantiation, saying it had 'no solid foundation in the word of God'. During this period he consulted with Bishop Tunstall, sharing, it seems, a desire for a 'middle way'.

In 1552 Tunstall appointed him to the parish of Norton-on-Tees, though he was not there for long. Gilpin emerged as a prominent preacher, and he was invited to preach before the court of Edward VI in January 1553. The sermon represented his final rejection of papal supremacy, though in moderate tones: 'I am sure no person ought to bear any malice or evil against his person, in speaking against his vice and iniquity...' It also included a rebuke to the king and his courtiers who were not present to hear the sermon:

'I am very sorry they should be absent, which ought to give example and encourage others to the hearing of God's word. But you will say, they have weighty matters in hand. Alas, hath God any greater business than this?… I will speak to their seats as if they were present.'

He then commented on the needs of the common people, both spiritual and physical. He attacked the spiritual neglect of people caused by the issues of pluralities and non-residence. He also addressed the issue of avarice, not least a problem in the court, for the poorest in society were robbed of what they had, and perhaps even turned off their farms or tenements.

The reasons behind his attacks are not clear from his previous career; however, he was not alone in his concern for the poor peasants of England, for other preachers made similar points. Towards the end of Mary's reign he was able to start to put his words into practice, even if he was by no means perfect in doing so.

The details of his appointments are not always clear, but by 1556 he was made Archdeacon of Durham and Rector of Easington, a joint appointment that was probably acceptable to him since the archdeacon's role was not a full-time one. He quickly sought to deal with clergy who did not take their parish duties seriously. From 1560 he was no longer archdeacon but Rector of Houghton-le-Spring, a position he held until his death in 1583/4, which came about through being knocked over by an ox in Durham marketplace.

Gilpin's work can be seen as an outworking of his two main concerns in his royal sermon: the spiritual and physical needs of the people.

One way in which he tried to meet spiritual needs was through his preaching tours of Northumberland. This was not new: Aidan and Cuthbert had done the same! Nor was Gilpin unique in his own time, but he was in the forefront of this development, and he showed some bravery in it. He was prepared to go where other preachers of his day feared to go, as the following story told of him at Rothbury Church implies.

Whilst preaching one Sunday morning, Gilpin observed a glove hanging up in the church and asked the sexton what it was for. The sexton told Gilpin that it was meant as a challenge to anyone who removed it. Gilpin asked the sexton to take the glove down, but not surprisingly he refused, fearing for his life. Gilpin therefore removed it himself, placed it in his breast pocket and continued with his sermon against the evil ways of his congregation. For some reason no one had the courage to challenge Bernard Gilpin.

His most significant long-term legacy was in education, especially through the foundation and endowment of Kepier Grammar School in 1574. Again, he was not unique in providing education, either on the small scale in his own rectory, or on the larger scale through the school. However, he was inspirational in gaining John Heath of Kepier as benefactor, supplemented by some of his income from his parish, and he provided educational expertise himself. Remember, this was a man who had spent some seventeen or eighteen years at Oxford, and was a notable scholar in Greek and Hebrew. Not surprisingly, then, the school gained a reputation for scriptural learning and the production of preachers, a key requirement in the Elizabethan Church of England.

He also attended to the very real physical needs of his parishioners. He was remembered for his great hospitality, putting some of his annual income of £400 to use in the feeding of the poor, particularly each Sunday from Michaelmas to Easter. He was concerned to develop farming in the parish, and if the harvest was bad he was ready to cancel the tithe he was owed.

At his death his substantial estate went mostly to the school and to the poor of the parish. His generosity is still celebrated in the 'Ox Roast' in the annual 'Houghton Feast', a week-long festival held each October.

Gilpin's holiness was shown in his willingness to challenge vested interests, in the clergy and even in the aristocracy. For him this did not mean abandoning his large income, but instead using it wisely and for the long-term good of the people around him. He is rightly celebrated for his generosity in immediate needs and his thoughtfulness in long-term educational needs.

Godric (c. 1065–1170)

Godric of Finchale was a hermit and popular medieval saint, though never formally canonized. He was born in Walpole in Norfolk and died at Finchale. His life was recorded by a contemporary monk, Reginald of Durham, and we have no means of checking the stories. However, they are fascinating tales and at the very least give an insight into the way holiness could be celebrated in the twelfth century.

According to Reginald, Godric was born into a humble family, to Ailward and Edwenna, 'both of slender rank and wealth, but abundant in righteousness and virtue'. He was a pedlar, then a sailor and entrepreneur, and he may have been the captain and owner of the ship that took Baldwin I of Jerusalem to Jaffa in 1102. After his years as a sailor, and in some versions a pirate, Godric is said to have gone to Lindisfarne, where he had a vision of St Cuthbert that changed his life.

From this point he devoted himself to serving God, and his voyages included pilgrimages to Rome and to St James Compostela in Spain. On his return to England he lived for two years with a hermit named Aelric. When Aelric died Godric made a second pilgrimage to Jerusalem, and he took the opportunity to learn more about the hermit's life in the desert there. Returning to England he first served as a doorkeeper at the hospital church of the nearby St Giles' Hospital on the edge of Durham City. He then persuaded the Bishop of Durham to grant him a place to live as a hermit at Finchale.

The record says that he lived at Finchale for the final sixty years of his life, occasionally meeting with visitors approved by Prior Roger of Durham. His life was centred on the monastic life of prayer and further contemplation in a context of penitence. This was a lonely existence, though he is remembered for his kindness towards the wild animals in the woods around him. Despite the challenges, he persevered and came to be loved by the peasants and monks who lived nearby.

He also wrote hymns, and his lyrics are amongst the oldest to use rhyme and measure rather than the alliteration found in Anglo-Saxon verse. They are the earliest English songs to survive with musical notation. He set his words to simple tunes that he claimed to receive in visions. Fragments of four of these tunes and texts have been preserved in the British Museum; they are hymns in honour of Christ, St Mary and St Nicholas.

After his death in 1170 his tomb became a shrine at which miracles of healing were performed, especially on women.

Godric's life, at least as we have it, displays a great contrast between the years of travel and action and the years of stillness and contemplation. This contrast is not a straightforward division between profane and holy, for he was drawn to God in the years of his activity and continued that life for some time. Perhaps the call to be holy will involve us in living as we are, externally at any rate, but being open to the possibility of new directions at any stage of our lives.

PLACES

St Michael's and All Angels, Houghton-le-Spring

The origins of this community probably lie before the Norman Conquest, but little is known until the building of a church by the Normans in the eleventh century. It has been much altered since; both inside and outside many detailed changes can be seen. This process of development has continued to the present day and is visible in windows commemorating the most famous rector of the parish, Bernard Gilpin. New windows were put in for both the 300th and the 400th anniversaries of his death, showing his continuing influence in the area, and the interest shown in his life and work.

St Laurence, Pittington

The church of St Laurence, Hallgarth, Pittington, is included as the last parish of Alexander Boddy; it is his and Mary's burial place. However, the building is also significant for two much older features.

The oldest part of the present church is the western end of the nave. From the north aisle, looking up at the top of the nave wall above the arches, what was the outside of the church in the twelfth century can be seen. The two small windows and the cornerstones of the original nave are a reminder of the simplicity of the early Norman building. The windows were later blocked and only rediscovered in the nineteenth century, along with rare twelfth-century wall paintings, showing scenes from the life of St Cuthbert.

The second important feature of St Laurence is the north arcade. Around 1180, during the time of Bishop Hugh de Puiset, the church was extended considerably. An aisle was added to the original north wall, and the decorated pillars and arches were added. It is believed that these were designed by the same architect who designed the Galilee Chapel in Durham Cathedral, and they offer a delightful precursor to a cathedral visit.

St Mary and St Cuthbert, Chester-le-Street

In 883, after seven years of wandering, the Community of St Cuthbert settled at Chester-le-Street with their most precious possessions: the body of Cuthbert and the Lindisfarne Gospels. They stayed for more than a century but perhaps did not expect to, for they seem to have had a timber church through all that time. Nonetheless, this was the cathedral of a huge diocese stretching from Edinburgh in Scotland to Teesside in northern England, and from the east to the west coasts of Britain. Important visitors and benefactors came because of the legends of the healing miracles attributed to Cuthbert's remains. Most notably, in 937 King Athelstan came to ask for Saint Cuthbert's assistance in a forthcoming battle with the Scots, bringing with him many gifts.

Around 950, the priest Aldred added his Anglo-Saxon translation, in the Northumbrian dialect, to the Lindisfarne Gospels, writing the words above the Latin text. This act of 'vandalism' has given us the oldest surviving version of the Bible in English and proved important in the time of Queen Elizabeth I in constructing the first dictionary of Old Anglo-Saxon and English.

The community left Chester-le-Street for Durham in 995, but about fifty years later the first stone church was built as a memorial to Cuthbert. The present building, dedicated to St Mary and St Cuthbert, dates from after 1100, with the oldest feature now the vestry. Like nearly all medieval churches, what we now have has been added to over the centuries, and the original plan is hard to find. It is believed that this is the site of the timber church and the first stone church, but any archaeological evidence is buried beneath today's building.

An unusual feature of the church is the tiny two-storey anchorage beside the west door at the base of the tower. Now the Anker's House Museum, it was, from 1383 to 1547, the dwelling-place of an anchorite. The anchorite, having been approved by the bishop, took monastic vows and was sealed in for the rest of his or her life. (The best-known English example is Julian of Norwich.) A small window allowed limited access and the passing in of food, and an angled slit in the interior wall formed a 'squint' through which the anchorite could observe the celebration of the Mass in the side chapel of the church.

The changes in the church building prompt reflection on various modes of Christian holy living: the early Community of St Cuthbert, in which priests, monks and lay people shared in the holy life together; the medieval parish church, which hosted a small community of ordained clergy; the solitary life of an anchorite, devoted to personal prayer and contemplation; and the present church, gathered from a wider community, seeking to live out the gospel in a world that is once again full of religious diversity. The variety of models over the years reminds us that the Christian faith has often had to adapt to the existing social conditions and then work out what holiness looks like. In that way our own time is no different.

Finchale Priory (pronounced 'finkle')

This comparatively small priory is in a scenic spot on the banks of the River Wear, about 4 miles from Durham. It began as a hermitage for St Godric, who lived a simple, solitary life in a crude hut for over fifty years. At the end of the twelfth century Finchale became a Benedictine priory, a daughter house of Durham Cathedral. The building work on the priory

began during the latter half of the thirteenth century, with many alterations and additions made over the next 300 years. There are still the fragments of the early twelfth-century stone chapel of St John the Baptist, built towards the end of St Godric's life, which is where he was finally buried. This became a local place of pilgrimage. About twenty years after his death, a small group of temporary buildings were erected for the first prior and his monks sent to establish the priory, and the ruins of these buildings are still visible.

Finchale was a small priory, probably of no more than four monks and a prior, and it was used by small groups of monks from Durham for a rest period. Its relative isolation would offer both a spiritual retreat and a healthier environment than the crowded conditions of the cathedral monastery in Durham.

Like the church at Chester-le-Street the changes to the site are very visible, from a solitary place of retreat for Godric, to a small priory, to a holiday home for Durham monks, to the present caravan park and working farm. Yet it remains an attractive spot and offers an opportunity to reflect on the impact we have had on God's creation.

Prayer

God of Godric, God of Gilpin,
You take people as they are,
with all their frailties and faith.

Grant us grace to hear your call:
the call to persevere,
the call to change,
the call to commit ourselves.

Grant us grace to receive the holiness of Jesus in the circumstances
of our lives.

Practicalities

From Monkwearmouth follow signs south over the River Wear for Durham. Take the A690 for Durham. Both Houghton-le-Spring and Pittington are just a short distance off the A690. If you wish to go to Chester-le-Street (and Finchale Priory) they can be reached directly from Houghton-le-Spring via the A1052 and the A183.

St Michael's and All Angels, Houghton-le-Spring

From Sunderland take the second turning for the town off the A690 and follow signs for the council offices, which are opposite the church. Car parking for the church is on the roadside.

Visits can be arranged by contacting the Church Office on 0191 512 1769.

http://www.stmichaels-hls.org.uk/

Refreshments are available in the town centre nearby.

St Laurence, Pittington

From the A690 take the Pittington turning. On entering the village go straight ahead at the crossroads and take the first left turn (approximately ½ mile). Turn right at the Hallgarth Manor Hotel and you will find the church at the end of the short road.

Car parking for the church is on the roadside. The church is open on Saturday afternoons from 2 p.m. to 4 p.m., May to September.

http://www.saint-laurence.org.uk/

Refreshments are available at the Hallgarth Manor Hotel, close to the church.

St Mary and St Cuthbert, Chester-le-Street

From Houghton-le-Spring take the A1052 and then the A183. From Pittington, go to the A1(M) and turn north, coming off after one junction (J62).

Park in one of the public car parks. The church is open from November until Easter, 10 a.m. to 12.30 p.m., Monday to Friday; from Easter to October, 10 a.m. to 3.30 p.m., Monday to Saturday. The museum is open from Easter Monday to the end of October, Monday to Saturday, from 10 a.m. to 3.30 p.m.

Opposite, in Church Chare, is the Parish Centre, which is open most of the time; call there if the main church building is closed.

http://www.maryandcuthbert.org.uk/

Refreshments are available in the town centre nearby.

Finchale Priory

Finchale Priory is reached by travelling south on the A167 to the northern edge of Durham, and following signs to the priory.

The priory is open Saturday and Sunday, 10 a.m.–4 p.m. At other times the ruins can be seen quite well from the perimeter fence.

http://www.english-heritage.org.uk/server/show/conProperty.129

Pilgrims on foot could use the Weardale Way from Wearmouth to Chester-le-Street, Finchale Priory and then into Durham. There is no convenient walk to Houghton-le-Spring and Pittington, but buses from Sunderland to Durham are frequent.

http://www.weardaleway.com/

Durham Cathedral:
Sign of Strength and Faith

This Day is focused on one of the great buildings of Britain, which is also a World Heritage Site. Inevitably there are riches here that cannot be covered in a book of this length so, should you have the opportunity to visit, do make use of other information available in the cathedral.

The cathedral is the last resting place of the remains of Cuthbert (see Day 1) and Bede (see Day 3), and possibly of King Oswald's head too (see Day 2). But the splendour of the building itself means that the emphasis for this visit is more on the place than on the people. So we begin with the story of the origins of the building itself – the opening of a biography of the building, if you like – and there is a description of a short tour. Also included are some of the less well-known stories linked to Durham Cathedral and its people.

PLACES

The origins of Durham Cathedral
Why did the Community of St Cuthbert move to Durham in 995? Our main source is the work of the Durham monk Symeon, who published his book on the origins of the church at Durham in the early 1100s.

According to Symeon, in 995 Bishop Ealdhun of Chester-le-Street had a vision that the community should flee with

Cuthbert's body because an attack was imminent; they went to Ripon, perhaps because Cuthbert had been guestmaster there for a time. The danger did not last long – no attacks are recorded for that year in other documents – and they set off on the return journey. On the way, not far to the east of Durham, the body came to a halt and could not be moved. They took this as a sign that the saint did not want to go back to Chester-le-Street, but they did not know where to go.

One later story tells of a milkmaid appearing with a red cow, the dun cow, and leading them to the peninsula. (A panel of the dun cow can be seen on the outside of the cathedral on the corner of the north transept.) In Symeon's version the community was called to pray and fast for three days, and a certain Eadmer received a revelation that they should go to Durham. There they went, and they made a little church of branches and placed Cuthbert's body in it.

Both stories are interesting, but leave us wondering why Durham was now favoured. We have no definite answers, but there is a plausible explanation. The Community of St Cuthbert was not a regular monastic community in the Benedictine sense, but one that contained lay and ordained folk, and included married clergy, and even a married bishop, all in order at that time. Their leader, Bishop Ealdhun, had a daughter Ecgfrida, who was married to Earl Uhtred, ruler of Bamburgh. Uhtred helped the community to clear the peninsula site and then build a church by supplying labour from the vast area between the Rivers Coquet and Tees. In other words, there was a political dimension in moving to Durham, strengthening the link between the community and the ruling family.

By the year 1000 the Community of St Cuthbert was well settled on the peninsula, with a substantial cathedral church, called the White Church, and was served by a community of clergy. By the time of the Norman Conquest in 1066 the Community of St Cuthbert had existed for nearly 400 years. It had survived and even flourished under a huge variety of systems: Northumbrian kings, earls of Bamburgh, Scandinavian kings of York, Saxon kings of Wessex. The successive bishops and the community had defended and extended their estates over this long period, and even a strong king like William the Conqueror had to appreciate their power, especially so far from his own centres of power.

In January 1069, however, William sent Robert Cumin to Northumbria to take charge. Once the force of 700 had entered Durham, Northumbrians from north of the Tyne came into the city and slaughtered the Normans in the narrow streets. It is unlikely that the bishop and community took part in this, but, fearing reprisals, they fled to Lindisfarne. True to his reputation, William sent another army north, but mist came upon it at Northallerton, interpreted as Cuthbert's protection, and the army did not make it to Durham.

Rebellion broke out across the country in 1069–70 and was put down ruthlessly. This was the period of the 'Harrowing of the North', with one source claiming that no village was inhabited between York and Durham. Durham itself was probably attacked in early 1070, as was St Paul's Church at Jarrow. When the community returned from Lindisfarne in March 1070, they were shocked by the plundering and so cleansed and rededicated the church.

A new bishop was appointed, Walcher, and he came in to reform the community, for it was not following the current Continental monastic best practice. Walcher himself was not a monk but began a process of change by introducing stricter liturgical practices. His successor, William of St Calais, furthered the reform of the community in 1083 by gathering monks from the re-founded monasteries at Monkwearmouth and Jarrow. In 1093 he laid the foundation of a new cathedral church; it was completed in just forty years and provides the essential structure of the present building.

To bolster their claims the new Norman bishops wanted to make use of the growing popular attachment to local saints, part of a wider European trend. In most parts of Britain it was sixth- and seventh-century saints who were promoted, testament to their continuing appeal.

A major way in which this was done was through the writing of new *Lives* (in Latin *Vitae*) of these saints. Around 1100 a new *Life of Cuthbert* appeared, with fifty-five coloured pictures, and it recorded seven new posthumous miracles. (Some pictures from this *Life* can be seen in a wall exhibition in the cloister.) The shrine of Cuthbert was created at the same time; in 1104, before the whole cathedral was finished, Cuthbert's body was moved with great ceremony to its new shrine at the east end of the cathedral. This became the heart of the cathedral until the Reformation and remains a special place on any pilgrimage to the cathedral.

A pilgrimage tour of the cathedral

There are many ways to encounter this great cathedral, and on the cathedral bookstall there is more information about other kinds of tours. Here is a simple tour that emphasizes the links with the stories told elsewhere in this guide and offers a few pointers to later developments.

1. *Palace Green, looking south*

Beginning outside gives a basic orientation of the building and how it was used by pilgrims in the medieval period. On the left is the east end, enclosing the key element of the shrine of St Cuthbert, completed in 1104. The first and main phase of building was finished by 1133. The Chapel of the Nine Altars, which now surrounds the

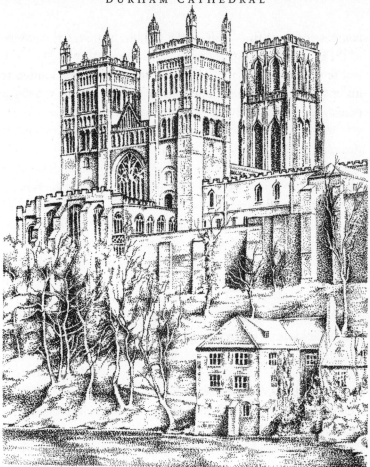

east end, was finished in 1274. To the right, the Galilee Chapel at the west end was finished in 1189, the western towers in 1226 and a central tower in 1262. This completed the building as it is now, apart from a rebuilding of the central tower in 1490.

2. *The font*

The font is symbolically important as the entry to the visible fellowship of the church; in Christ believers are baptized into new relationships that break down old barriers. It is ironic that here there is a black marble line, from the monastic period – a line over which women could not go. It was claimed that Cuthbert did not want women near his tomb. This is a slur on the saint, who is recorded as having good relationships with women, and it reflects a later generation's attempt to make use of his memory for their own purposes.

Thus at this point the pilgrimage within the cathedral symbolizes the beginning of the spiritual life, which unfolds through the building. Here too is unity in Christ, marked in the baptism common to all Christians. Whilst this building is cared for by one particular group, it is open to all and many find a sense of belonging here.

3. *In front of the font, looking east down the nave*
Looking east one sees the massive pillars, marching down the church, holding up the first large stone vault built in England. The precision of the pillars, their detailed decoration and the scale of the nave are calculated to give a sense not only of God's majesty, but also of humanity's place in the scheme of things – small in comparison to the God of creation, but not overwhelmed, having significance in the world.

Medieval pilgrims would have been captivated by the colour in the building, with its painted walls and ceilings. In our day colour comes from stained glass and increasingly from banners. To the north is the modern window of the Last Supper – a sign of God's provision in Christ.

Going east recapitulates the route of the medieval pilgrims, moving from the starting point of the font, making their way through the stages of the building, and ending at the shrine of Cuthbert. As those early pilgrims moved through the building they would have been very aware of the difference between their own small homes and this great house of God. Like them, visitors today marvel at the skill and devotion that the builders gave over their lifetimes to make possible this building. Here is an opportunity to consider your own life experiences that need to be brought to God.

4. *The crossing*

At the crossing the usual shape of medieval churches as a cross is clear. The scale of the tower above offers a further opportunity to appreciate the massive task of constructing this building – the skill, dedication and worship involved.

This is another transitional point in the cathedral, with the screen representing the way in which ordinary people were kept separate from the life of the religious, monastic community in the building, at least until the Reformation. The present screen is nineteenth century but replaces an earlier one. In pre-Reformation times there was a solid screen, so that the monks could pray in relative privacy.

5. *The quire (or choir)*

This was where the monks of the Benedictine monastery prayed seven times a day and where Morning and Evening Prayer has been said daily since the Reformation. It is the praying heart of the cathedral, and the cathedral community see it as the centre of their mission. It may prompt us to consider the ways in which our own communities make prayer the centre of their mission.

The current appearance owes much to Bishop Cosin, who introduced the dark oak choir stalls after the Restoration of the monarchy in 1660.

The ambiguity of church power is also represented: here is the tomb of Bishop Hatfield, perhaps the most powerful of all the so-called prince-bishops. Above his tomb is the throne of the bishop, still used in the enthronement ceremony for new Bishops of Durham. It was deliberately constructed as the highest throne of Western Christendom, higher even than that of St Peter's Rome. It indicates how the prince-bishops saw themselves. It was also necessary for Cuthbert and his contemporaries to engage with the political powers of their own day, but this deliberate aggrandizement seems far removed from the personal simplicity and humility of Cuthbert (see Day 1).

6. *The feretory (shrine of Cuthbert)*

The purpose of this whole building is to encourage the worship of God, and for several centuries that worship was focused on the shrine of Cuthbert, the first part of the building to be finished. In the medieval period the shrine was one of the most important in England, and it became very rich with the gifts of the pilgrims. The Lindisfarne Gospels were held here, for use at special services rather than for everyday Bible readings.

The shrine was dismantled at the Reformation and the gold, jewels and Gospels were removed. The shrine is now a simple stone slab, with the inscription *Cuthbertus*, and it remains the emotional heart of the building for many people in the region. Cuthbert's bones are still here, along with the head of Oswald, it is believed, and many other bones that were brought here from Lindisfarne over a millennium ago.

In recent times the cathedral has highlighted its role as the shrine of Cuthbert and added further decoration to the shrine and to other focal points in the Chapel of the Nine Altars, such as the modern icon of St Hilda (see Day 7). These recent additions to the cathedral are a sign of the renewed interest in our forebears in the faith.

This tour ends in the Galilee Chapel at the west end.

7. *Galilee Chapel*

This chapel was added to the cathedral in the late twelfth century. Its name comes about as the place in which liturgical processions began and ended, echoing the beginning and ending of Jesus' ministry in Galilee. Here is a good place to end this short pilgrimage around the cathedral.

The most important feature is, of course, the tomb of Bede (see Day 3). This too was once a rich shrine, but its present simplicity better reflects the humble monk-scholar. There is usually scope for quiet reflection in this part of the cathedral.

If possible it is also good to visit other parts of the cathedral, including the cloister – important in the monastic origins of Durham – and the various exhibitions around the cloister. The Monks' Dormitory is a wonderful space enclosed by a hammer-beam roof and containing an important collection of stone crosses and other early Christian artefacts. The Treasury houses the wooden coffin of Cuthbert and his richly jewelled pectoral cross. On the other side of the cloister there are audio-visual displays: 'The Story of Saint Cuthbert and Durham Cathedral' and 'Building the Church'.

PEOPLE

Here we have the brief telling of two lives from the period in which the present cathedral was built. Inevitably we tend to know only about exceptional people, but they do at least illustrate two ways in which people sought to live holy, Christian lives, the first as a mother and a queen(!), and the second as a monk. Their very different, though briefly connected, lives remind us that there are many ways to follow Christ.

Queen Margaret of Scotland (1046–93)

Queen Margaret of Scotland is celebrated in the cathedral in a striking modern painting by Paula Rego sited at the Queen Margaret Altar in the Chapel of the Nine Altars. She is thought to have been present with her husband, King Malcolm III, when the foundation stone of Durham was laid in August 1093. Her confessor, friend and first biographer was Durham's Prior Turgot. Indeed, both the prior and the king laid foundation stones for the cathedral, with Queen Margaret a clear link between them.

She had been born into the Anglo-Saxon royal house of England in 1046, but was educated in Hungary whilst in exile after the Danish king Canute over-ran England. Her brother was briefly considered as an alternative king to William the Conqueror, but this only led to a second exile, this time at the court of Malcolm III of Scotland. After Malcolm's persistent wooing Margaret married him three years later, and they were a happy couple until their deaths in 1093.

Margaret was renowned as a civilizing influence on the court, bringing a knowledge of Continental culture and practices, and especially a concern for religious observance. She encouraged the use of Latin, promoted time off from menial work on Sundays and founded many monasteries and churches; she and Malcolm were great benefactors of Durham Cathedral. She was the instigator of the Queen's Ferry over the River Forth to ensure that pilgrimages could reach the shrine of St Andrew. She was also known for her care for the poor and for her seriousness in prayer and fasting.

She and Malcolm had eight children, amongst them David, who is shown in the cathedral painting. He went on to become one of the greatest kings of Scotland and himself founded many more churches and monasteries. During this time there was a special bond between the Scottish royal family and Durham, and the city was generally spared when the rest of the region was being raided by Scottish armies.

Margaret died in 1093 after hearing of the deaths of Malcolm and her eldest son at the battle of Alnwick. She was buried in Dunfermline Abbey, and reports of miracles eventually led to her formal canonization as a saint in 1250. The monks of Durham had also been impressed by her, and obtained relics of some of her hair and a tooth!

The cathedral painting symbolizes the hard life she led – in exile twice, and an asylum seeker in Scotland – and her work over many years to reform the church in Scotland. Her holiness was lived out in both need and relative plenty, in danger and security; it took courage and determination. She sought to make good use of the position she attained as queen, and her example challenges us all in the holy use of the gifts and influence we have.

Symeon (died around 1128)

Of all the monks who lived in Durham after its rebuilding until the Reformation, one of the most informative was the writer Symeon. He seems to have arrived in Durham around 1091, when Bishop William returned from exile. Symeon himself was probably from Normandy but made his new home in Durham. He was brought in order to write documents for the bishop and the community. This was a key task, as all documents were handwritten; Symeon was entrusted with some of the most important of their texts, such as the *Life of Cuthbert*, the *History of Saint Cuthbert*, and various histories of the community. Indeed, he did his copying so well that some of his personal works are the earliest versions we have of these historic documents.

It is thanks to Symeon's work as a historian that we know how the Community of St Cuthbert came to leave its home on Holy Island, and eventually arrive in Durham. He is the one who recorded the story of the vision given to Eadmer, as well as the historical information about the ruling families, which helps us to reconstruct some of the power games that occurred. His history ends with the story of the turbulent changes of the eleventh century, before and after the Norman Conquest.

Symeon is not known for any special holiness of life, but rather he is included here to remind us of the many men and women who took vows as monks and nuns in order to live out the Christian life in that way, forsaking family and earthly fortune. Of course we are very aware of the ways in which this calling was abused, and we think we understand how the Reformation was necessary in order to rid the church of parasitic and corrupt religious orders. There is some truth in this condemnation, but Symeon stands for the faithful commitment of many thousands of unknown individuals to a life of prayer, caring and practical work for others. In our own day there are groups around the world rediscovering the value of community and shared worship, witnessing to the continuing worth of the monastic life in traditional and newer forms. Symeon's life offers the opportunity to reflect on the deep commitments made in our lives – to God and to others.

Prayer

Gracious and holy Father,
Give us wisdom to perceive you,
Intelligence to understand you,
Diligence to seek you,
Patience to wait for you,
Eyes to behold you,
A heart to meditate on you,
And a life to proclaim you,
Through the power of the Spirit of Jesus Christ our Lord.

A BENEDICTINE PRAYER

Practicalities

Durham Cathedral

Durham is well signed by road and can be easily reached by train and by bus. If arriving for the day car users would do well to use one of the Park & Ride schemes, though there is parking signed near the centre of the city. The cathedral is signed for pedestrians, and there is a bus available from the bus and train stations and from other stops in the centre.

The cathedral is open every day until 6 p.m., Monday to Saturday, and 5.30 p.m. on Sunday. Times for worship and private prayer are 7.30 a.m.–9.30 a.m., Monday to Saturday; 7.45 a.m.–12.30 p.m. on Sunday.

http://www.durhamcathedral.co.uk/

Refreshments are available in the cathedral refectory.

Other places

Auckland Castle and Chapel, Bishop Auckland: Auckland Castle has been the home of the Bishop of Durham for many centuries. It has its own chapel within the grounds, and the entire estate is set in parkland and can be found on the east side of the marketplace in Bishop Auckland. There is a charge to enter the castle, but the deer park is free from dawn until dusk. Main opening hours are from Easter Monday to end of September: Sundays and Mondays from 2 p.m. to 5 p.m. For further details check the website:

http://www.auckland-castle.co.uk/

Escomb Saxon Church: A few miles south-west of Durham, just beyond Bishop Auckland, is an unusual Anglo-Saxon church at Escomb. It was built around 670, and much of the stonework came from the remains of the nearby Roman fort at Binchester. Now restored, it is one of the finest examples of early Christian architecture in northern Europe. This small atmospheric church can be visited at any reasonable time during the day. For more information visit the website:

http://www.escombsaxonchurch.com/

Durham Dales and Methodism: *Holiness in Rough Times*

This Day is focused on more recent holy people, who were part of the Methodist Revival in the eighteenth century. Newcastle and the north-east was an important region for John Wesley, and he made nearly fifty visits during his travelling ministry from 1742 to 1790. So many visits means that there are a number of places associated with Wesley and of course many stories of his ministry in the region. Our selection concentrates on his work in the northern Dales, as there are some interesting places that have not yet been featured in this pilgrimage. It also allows us to hear of two less famous Methodist preachers, who gave a great deal of time, energy and love to sharing their faith with the farmers and miners who lived and worked in the Dales.

PEOPLE

John Wesley (1703–91)

John Wesley was born into a religious family. His father Samuel was a Church of England clergyman, and his mother Susanna was a devout follower of Christ, instilling Christian love and discipline into her children. Along with his brother Charles he formed a Holy Club whilst at the University of Oxford, a prototype for the class meetings they developed later in the

Methodist Movement. They were both ordained in the Church of England, and attempted missionary work in North America without much success. Returning to England Charles and then John experienced a conversion of heart in 1738 and devoted themselves to evangelistic work for the rest of their lives.

John Wesley came to Newcastle for the first time in May 1742. He was appalled and moved by the poverty, drunkenness and bad behaviour he saw. He preached on what is now the quayside on Sunday, 30 May at 7 a.m.:

'At seven I walked down to Sandgate, the poorest and most contemptible part of the town; and, standing at the end of the street with John Taylor, began to sing the hundredth Psalm. Three or four people came out to see what was the matter; who soon increased to four or five hundred.' (This and subsequent extracts are from Wesley's Journals.*)*

He preached again at 5 p.m., and people were moved by his preaching, many urging him to stay longer:

'The word of God which I set before them was, "I will heal their backsliding, I will love them freely." After preaching, the poor people were ready to tread me under foot, out of pure love and kindness. It was some time before I could possibly get out of the press. I then went back another way than I came; but several were got to our inn before me; by whom I was vehemently importuned to stay with them, at least, a few days; or, however, one day more.'

However, he was unable to stay at this time, although Newcastle and the region soon became important in his work. Wesley regularly travelled a triangle from London to Bristol and up to Newcastle, giving him the opportunity to visit many places on the way.

At this time the main occupations in the Dales of the north-east (Weardale, Teesdale, Swaledale, Allendale, Wensleydale) were hill farming and lead mining. Lead miners had a distinctive pattern of working in groups of four to eight men, who formed a small cooperative, sharing tasks and wages, and engaging in discussion, often on major philosophical and political topics. This gave them an independence of spirit and mind and inclined them towards Methodism, with its emphasis on personal salvation and responsibility.

Wesley's many visits to the Dales were just for a day or two at a time, but he found a responsive audience, and other local preachers stayed to continue and develop his work. His first contact with the lead-mining community was at Blanchland, on the River Derwent, in 1747. When he prayed in the churchyard, 'all the congregation kneeled down on the grass. They were gathered out of the lead-mines from all parts; many from Allendale, six miles off. A row of little children sat under the opposite wall, all quiet and still.'

His hope was for God to 'make this wilderness sing for joy', and he returned the following year, extending his visit to Allendale itself, then a significant centre for mining. Although Wesley spent a lot of time in the north-east, he mostly visited the towns, where he could meet larger numbers of people; much of his travelling within the Dales was in fact getting him from one town to another and making use of the journey to preach where he might. It has been estimated that in over fifty years of travelling, he did not spend much more than two months in the northern Dales of Wensleydale, Swaledale, Teesdale, Weardale, Allendale and Derwentdale. Yet there are chapels all over the Dales! This in itself is a clear demonstration that the growth of Methodism depended on many people, and two stories of such men follow.

Before we turn to these other stories, in thinking about Wesley's ministry and his approach to holiness, there are some parallels to the work of Aidan (see Day 1). They both began with a passion for God: Wesley spent his early life in his search for God and in his desire to live a holy life. After his conversion of heart he was wholly committed in his desire to travel to preach the gospel, even to the extent of ruining his ill-advised marriage (not to be recommended!).

Like Aidan he put people before possessions and lived frugally: for example, the room he used in the Orphan House in Newcastle was a simple, even austere, affair, and he delighted in sleeping outdoors into his seventies, when finally he had to give it up through ill health. As his fame grew, his writings sold very widely and his income was enormous, but most of it he gave away, aiming to live on the same amount throughout his life.

We saw how Aidan moved with ease between the layers of his society, and John Wesley did the same with his, even though he saw his primary calling as being to the poor and needy who were neglected by most of the established church at the time. But he and Charles recognized the value of help from wealthier supporters and from local leaders, and as Oxford-educated clergy they were perfectly capable of moving in those circles. What is more to be wondered at is the way in which they were able to relate to working men and women with whom socially they had little in common; Wesley's emphasis on simple living seems to have been a factor.

There is no evidence that Wesley drew on Aidan's example, but the similarities arise from their reflection on the pattern of Jesus in the Gospels. The connection between Wesley and Aidan in this regard is an encouragement to us to also follow Christ in holy living.

Christopher Hopper (1722–1802)

Christopher Hopper became one of the first evangelists and establishers of Methodist societies in the Dales after his early conversion. He was born and brought up at Ryton in County Durham on the south bank of the River Tyne, and from the age of fifteen he worked as a driver on the wagon-ways between the coal pits and the Tyne.

As early as 1743 he was converted and became a leader of the Methodist Society at Low Spen near Newcastle. He received invitations to preach in Blanchland, Prudhoe, Durham and Sunderland, though sometimes he met violent opposition. After his marriage in 1745 he moved with his wife Jane to the preacher's house at Sheephill, near Burnopfield. He had Quaker friends in the Dales, and this gave him the opportunity to preach in Allendale in 1747 before Wesley visited. A second visit led him and Jane to move there in 1748, into the home of the Broadwood family, Quakers who lived at Hindley Hall, near Keenley. The dale had a much larger population then, though the inhabitants had a precarious living from hill farming and lead mining. When Wesley came in July 1748 he also stayed with the Broadwoods and was able to build on the work already done by Hopper.

Hindley Hall became a regular stopping place for Wesley, and the second chapel in the north-east was built here. From this new base Hopper also travelled widely as a preacher. He not only established societies in the northern Dales but also went to Bradford, Liverpool and Manchester, and he accompanied Wesley on visits to Ireland and Scotland. (The chapel at Keenley is still in use and can be visited.)

Later in life Hopper was appointed President of the Methodist Conference at Bristol in 1780, the only person to hold this position other than Wesley during Wesley's lifetime. At his funeral the preacher said of him: he was 'a good man, full of faith, and mighty in scriptures. God greatly blessed his word both to saints and sinners; graciously banished all his fears, and made him as bold as a lion in the face of all his dangers.'

Jacob Rowell (died 1784)

Jacob Rowell was a young man brought up in Allendale, whose main interest was in cockfighting. On his way to a cockfight in December 1747, however, he found himself on the edge of a crowd listening to Christopher Hopper. Something in Hopper's words convinced him of the need to turn to Christ, and before long Rowell was working with Hopper, forming the new Methodist Society in the dale. Over time Allendale became part of the huge Dales Circuit, covering the area from Swaledale to Tynedale, and Darlington to Penrith. Rowell worked in Weardale as well as Allendale, becoming an itinerant minister in 1749 and continuing Hopper's work for forty years. Eventually he covered the entire circuit, travelling over the hills into remote settlements high in the Pennines, rather as Cuthbert (see Day 1) and Gilpin (see Day 4) had done in earlier centuries. Rowell was once asked by John Wesley to preach at the annual national Methodist Conference, and after that he was put in charge of the circuit. Here was a man not well known after his death, but representative of the many unknown people who put into practice the vision of a great leader like Wesley. His faithfulness and commitment were important in bringing holiness to the lives of the farmers and miners of the northern Dales.

PLACES

High House Chapel, Ireshopeburn, Weardale

High House Chapel is one of the oldest Methodist chapels in the world to be in continuous weekly use since its foundation in

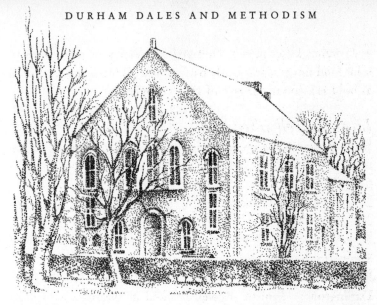

1760, and it is one of only four chapels listed by Simon Jenkins in his book *England's Thousand Best Churches*. Wesley preached here thirteen times, between 1752 (before the chapel had been built) and 1788. His second visit in 1761 enabled him to persuade the members of the Methodist Society not to leave the Church of England, whilst in 1772 he recorded details of a great revival of faith in 1771:

'they met every night for singing and prayer... Those who were strangers to God, felt, as it were, a sword in their bones, constraining them to roar aloud. Those who knew God were filled with joy unspeakable, and were almost equally loud in praise and thanksgiving.' (Wesley's Journal, *4 June 1772)*

Two years later some had fallen away, but Wesley came with further encouragement, and over the next few years he was delighted with this 'lovely congregation' (*Journal*, 12 May 1779). What now seems a sleepy place was once a busy industrial location, in which people found faith in God and wanted to live holy lives.

The interior is a good example of a chapel with surrounding galleries and a prominent central pulpit. Next door is a small folk museum, including a dedicated Wesley room, an 1870 period Weardale cottage room, local history displays and a superb collection of local crystallized minerals.

Newbiggin-in-Teesdale Methodist Chapel

This simple building is believed to be the oldest Methodist chapel in continuous use, from 1759. Inside is a display of Methodism and local history, including lead mining, and a pulpit from which John Wesley preached. His first visit in 1772 was not a great success, as he recorded in his 2 June *Journal* entry: 'We rode to Newbiggin in Teesdale. The people were deeply attentive but I think not deeply affected.' He found better things in Weardale, as recorded above.

An energetic day on his horse in the summer of 1784 took him from Barnard Castle to Cotherstone and Newbiggin:

'We rode through wind and rain to Newbiggin in Teesdale. Being but a poor horseman and having a rough horse, I had the strength for my journey and none to spare; but after resting awhile I preached without weariness.' (Journal, *10 June 1784*)

It was then 'over the great mountain into Weardale'. Wesley's continuing energy in his late seventies is remarkable, though it may be that he did not have much of an audience. The response in Newbiggin was not as positive as that in Ireshopeburn in Weardale.

Prayer

This is the traditional Methodist Covenant Prayer, generally used at the first service of the New Year, in a serious commitment to following and serving God.

I am no longer my own but yours.
Put me to what you will,
rank me with whom you will;
put me to doing,
put me to suffering;
let me be employed for you,
or laid aside for you,
exalted for you,
or brought low for you;
let me be full,
let me be empty,
let me have all things,
let me have nothing:
I freely and wholeheartedly yield all things
to your pleasure and disposal.
And now, glorious and blessed God,
Father, Son and Holy Spirit,
you are mine and I am yours.

Practicalities

High House Chapel, Ireshopeburn, Weardale

The chapel is found by following the main A689 road up Weardale, just west of the village of St John's Chapel.

Opening times are 2 p.m.–5 p.m., Wednesday to Sunday in May, June, July and September; 2 p.m.–5 p.m. at Easter and Bank Holidays; and every afternoon in August.

Parking is permitted at The Weardale Inn, 50 metres east of the chapel.
http://www.weardalemuseum.co.uk/

Newbiggin-in-Teesdale Methodist Chapel

The chapel can be reached by going over Wesley's 'great mountain' on the minor road from St John's Chapel to Langdon Beck and then travelling east down Teesdale. It is on the B6277 road, west of Middleton-on-Tees.

It is open on Wednesday afternoons from May Bank Holiday to August Bank Holiday, 2 p.m.–4 p.m. A key is available at other times, with the list of key holders on the chapel door. Nearby parking available.

Other places

Nenthead and Middleton: These villages are living reminders of the important Quaker connections in this area. Nenthead is the highest village in England, up in the Pennines, and it developed around lead mines. There are still many buildings put up by the Quaker London Lead Mining Company, as well as the museum of the recent Nenthead Mines Heritage Centre. Middleton-in-Teesdale was home to the headquarters of the London Lead Mining Company and has good tourist facilities.

Killhope Mining Centre: Killhope is the most complete lead-mining site in Britain. Restoration of the machinery is continuing. It is set in the moors at the top of Weardale and offers a glimpse into the harshness of life for lead miners in the nineteenth century and the conditions in which the early Methodists lived.

DAY 7

Hartlepool and Whitby: *Homes for a Woman of Vision*

This final Day is focused on Hilda, the founder of the original Whitby Abbey in 651 and its abbess for nearly thirty years. She was a remarkable woman who drew on both Roman and Irish understandings of Christianity, and she was held in high esteem by many church leaders, from Aidan to Cuthbert. Before going to Whitby, she was abbess of a smaller monastery at Hartlepool, and a few remains can be found on the headland there. She hosted the Synod of Whitby, which determined that the church in Northumbria would follow Roman and Continental practices in dating Easter: in the Appendix, I offer my thoughts on how we understand the significance of the synod – still a controversial subject.

We also hear the story of Cedd, who was trained on Lindisfarne, served as a missionary in several parts of England, including Essex, and died at Lastingham. And we hear of Reinfrid, a Norman knight turned monk, who helped to re-found a monastery at Whitby after the Norman Conquest. Space does not permit full descriptions of Lastingham or of Rievaulx Abbey, with its important abbot Aelred, but there are a few details of these places at the end.

PEOPLE

Hilda (614–80)

Hilda is best known for founding, in 657, the double monastery at Whitby, a place that drew on the Roman and Irish traditions of Christianity. Virtually all we know about her is in two chapters of Bede's *Ecclesiastical History* (Book 4, Chapters 23 and 24), along with some scanty archaeological material.

She was born in 614, into the ruling family of Deira, roughly modern-day Yorkshire. She was a great-niece of King Edwin, who became bretwalda (high king) of the English in the 620s. Her father was Hereric, nephew to Edwin, and her mother Breguswith, both of whom were members of the royal family of Deira. Hilda is thought to mean 'maid of war, or battle'. At the time of her birth Northumbria was ruled by Ethelfrith of the royal family of Bernicia, based in Bamburgh. It was a tough period, though, for her father was in exile when she was very young, and he was killed by poisoning.

When she was young her family regained the kingdom of Northumbria, and her great-uncle Edwin became king in 616. If he had any Christian faith at this time it was not made public (there are divergent records on this). It is more likely that he ruled as a pagan for the first years of his reign, though Bede interpreted Edwin's success as due to God's favour.

The first mission to convert the Northumbrians came about later because Edwin wanted to make an alliance with the powerful Kentish kingdom, in support of his bid to be overlord. His first wife had died and he took the opportunity to link himself with Kent through marriage. However, he was only allowed to marry their princess Ethelberga if he agreed to receiving her Christian advisers and priests. Amongst them was Bishop Paulinus. We may fairly imagine Hilda, now aged eleven, and herself fast approaching marriageable age, watching with considerable interest.

Edwin remained cautious about the Christian faith, and Paulinus made little headway. Then, in 626, a suicide mission was sent to Edwin by the King of the West Saxons on Easter Day. He was protected by his favourite counsellor, who placed his body in the way of the poisoned dagger; after wounding the king and killing yet another man the assassin was killed. The same day the queen gave birth prematurely, but she and the child survived. Paulinus interpreted the events as evidence of the Christian God's protection, and Edwin was sufficiently convinced to have his newborn daughter, Eanfled, baptized along with twelve of her household on the following Pentecost.

Edwin himself held back from baptism until he had defeated the King of the West Saxons. Having proved this God in battle he was baptized at York the following Easter, along with many of his household, including Hilda, now aged thirteen.

Edwin then used his influence over the bishops, the construction of Christian centres, and the deployment of clergy as means of control in his kingdom. Bede saw this as a golden age in which there was peace, and people could walk from one side of the kingdom to the other without fear. Even if we must allow for some exaggeration this will have given the young Hilda a positive view of the Christian faith.

Just a few years later, in 633, Edwin was killed at the battle of Hatfield (south Yorkshire). Edwin's adult sons were killed, whilst the queen, his younger children by Ethelberga and his grandson were taken south by Paulinus for protection. We are not told what happened to Hilda, but it is possible she was taken south with Paulinus. Her older sister Hereswith had married the King of the East Anglians, and another possibility is that she went to the court there. Given that Hilda was nineteen by now, her apparently unmarried status may suggest that she was already keen to pursue the religious life.

We are not told anything more about her until 647. That year, at the age of thirty-three, she responded to a call to the monastic life, and was encouraged in this by Aidan. Perhaps she had returned to Northumbria by this stage under the rule of Oswald and then Oswy and Oswin, for the mother of Oswald and Oswy was also the sister of Edwin.

Hilda first went to East Anglia and intended to go to a French convent, at Chelles near Paris, joining her widowed sister there. But Aidan called her back to Northumbria and she was given a hide of land on the north bank of the Wear, thus pre-dating Benedict Biscop's monastery of St Peter's Wearmouth. Forming a small community, she stayed there a year.

Following the departure of its founding abbess she was next called to lead the monastery at Hartlepool, a daughter house of Lindisfarne, and established it firmly during her nine years of leadership. All this was under the oversight of Aidan.

According to Bede, Aidan and other devout men admired her wisdom and would visit there to offer their guidance.

In 657 Hilda founded the double monastery at Whitby at the prompting of King Oswy. Up to this point the most important monastery in Northumbria had been Lindisfarne, founded under Oswald. Following the assassination of Oswin, King of Deira, Oswy needed to assert his authority over the southern kingdom. He turned to Hilda as the existing pre-eminent leader of a monastery in that part of Northumbria. Her royal pedigree ensured her recognition socially, and her piety and wisdom ensured her spiritual recognition.

Whitby was a double monastery; that is, containing men and women living under vows. This may have had some link to Irish monasticism in that many of their foundations might be described as Christian villages, with men, women and children. However, the strongest link was to other double monasteries in northern Gaul, or Francia, where they were something of a speciality. Amongst them was Chelles, where Hereswith had gone and Hilda had intended to go. In fact Bede records that from 640 many prospective nuns went to Francia because there were few monasteries in England. Hereswith and Hilda were part of a wider movement.

As happened elsewhere, Whitby became a centre of learning, the mother monastery of a network of smaller foundations, a cooperative venture between the secular ruler and religious leaders.

Bede emphasizes how it followed the example of the primitive church in four ways, all of them dependent on Hilda's own devotion and example:

1. Hilda 'taught the observance of righteousness, mercy, purity and other virtues, but especially of peace and charity'. The emphasis on peace and charity seems to reflect Bede's own knowledge that these qualities were not automatically or easily achieved in a closed community. At her death Hilda urged her community to keep the 'gospel peace amongst themselves'. For this was a community of people of both low and the highest social standings, and in life outside the monastery the hierarchy was very strict.

2. Strongly reminiscent of the primitive church was the community's attitude to possessions, a feature picked up from Aidan's example, as well as a reflection on the church described in Acts 2:44–45; in Bede's words, 'no one was rich, no one was needy, for everything was held in common, and nothing was considered to be anyone's personal possessions' (*Ecclesiastical History*, Book 4, Chapter 23).

3. Ordinary folk and nobles consulted Hilda for advice, 'so great was her prudence'. Again, there was a democratic flavour to the comment, indicating her willingness and ability to speak with all classes of society.

4. Part of the eclipsing of Lindisfarne at this period was the way in which Hilda established Whitby as a place of learning. This meant the 'thorough study of the Scriptures', something close to Bede's own heart, and engaging in good works.

Thus she trained many nuns, priests and no fewer than five bishops, including Wilfrid.

As with Aidan, a significant part of Hilda's influence came through her personal example of holy living, an influence that spread beyond her own communities to many others who heard accounts of her life.

A story from the last year of her life illustrates her gift of encouragement.

Caedmon was a keeper of animals for the monastery who discovered a gift for writing poetry. One evening there was a feast at which the harp was being passed round for each person to sing. Caedmon always left early as he was unable to sing, but this time, after fulfilling his duties in the stables and settling for sleep, he had a dream. A man called to him to sing – to sing of creation, in the English language, beginning:

Praise we the Fashioner now of Heaven's fabric
The majesty of his might and his mind's wisdom

In the morning Caedmon added further verses, took them to his superior, the reeve, who took him to Hilda herself. With others, she agreed this was a gift from God, and she encouraged

Caedmon to take monastic vows in order to use this gift in writing songs for the community. According to Bede, he wrote songs on the whole story of the Bible, from creation, through the history of Israel, to the life, death and resurrection of Jesus and the final judgment. Sadly none of these have survived.

In 674, Hilda, aged sixty, became seriously ill, racked by a 'burning fever'; however, she continued to teach and lead her community until her death in 680. Her saintly life was confirmed for her contemporaries by a vision granted to a nun called Begu, who lived at a daughter house of Whitby called Hackness. Whilst at rest she heard in her mind the bell used when any of the sisters died. Then she saw a great light, which she perceived as the soul of Hilda ascending to heaven. The next day it was found to have been the very time at which Hilda had died. Thus was Hilda's sanctity authenticated.

In Hilda we see a woman who did not deny her royal background but worked with the needs of her society to find out how Christianity would both fit into their culture and re-shape it. Her gifts of wisdom, encouragement and teaching all played a part in this. Like others, Bede admired her evident holiness, seen because her lifestyle and teaching were of a piece.

Cedd (died 664)

Cedd was the oldest of four Anglo-Saxon brothers, born in Northumbria and in the first generation of native monks and priests trained by Aidan. Their lives show how Christian holiness was developed and lived out in demanding times.

The four brothers – Cedd, Cynibil, Caelin and Chad – all trained on Holy Island under Aidan's leadership. Most unusually, all became priests and Cedd and then Chad were also bishops. After Aidan's death Cedd was chosen by King Oswy to be one of four priests on a mission in 653 to the Middle Angles, preaching and baptizing. This proved successful and he was quickly sent on a second mission, this time to Essex, after the conversion of Sigbert, King of the East Saxons.

This clearly went well, for in 654 he was recalled to Holy Island and consecrated by Bishop Finan as Bishop of the East Saxons. Returning to Essex, probably by sea, Cedd founded several churches, baptizing converts, and founded two monasteries – at Bradwell-on-Sea and at Tilbury. Bede emphasizes the difficulty of founding monasteries amongst 'untutored folk', but Cedd tried to teach them monastic discipline.

Cedd continued to travel back to Northumbria to preach and he renewed his friendship with King Ethelwald , the sub-king of Deira and the son of King Oswald. Their friendship was aided by Cedd's brother Caelin, who was the king's chaplain. The king asked Cedd to found a monastery on his lands as a place for his own burial. Cedd chose a place in the remote hills (as it seemed to Bede), and he founded his third monastery at Lastingham on the southern edge of the North York Moors.

Rather helpfully to us, Bede gives more detail of the spiritual preparation in the founding of this monastery than that of any other. So we learn that Cedd deliberately chose a place more suitable for robbers and wild beasts in order to purify it for God. He achieved this by praying and fasting on the site throughout Lent. He fasted each day until evening (except for Sundays), and even then ate only a little bread, egg and watered milk. This was how he had been trained on Holy Island: before any monastery or church was built the site was dedicated in prayer and fasting. Here was the practice of the Irish church and of Aidan in particular still being lived out, so that a holy person might create a new holy place.

Cedd was a prominent person at the Synod of Whitby, as a supporter of the Irish side. However, he was clearly trusted by all, for he was the key interpreter for both parties. As a result of the meeting he accepted the Roman argument over the dating of Easter, and is the only person named as doing so, though many other people did too. His leadership in this matter is thus made obvious, but sadly it was not to last for long as he caught and died from the plague when visiting Lastingham and was buried there.

He was succeeded by Chad as abbot, and the monastery survived the attack of plague. After Cedd's death about thirty of his monks came from Essex to be with their founder in life and death, but all but one died of the plague very soon after their arrival. Later, when life was more settled, a stone church was built to commemorate Cedd, and the church remains a special place, with a peaceful atmosphere. He lived a life that was committed to God and encouraged others to know God and live holy lives themselves.

Reinfrid (died around 1087)

Many of the holy people in this book lived in the seventh century and were made famous by Bede. This is the moving story of Reinfrid – an invading Norman knight turned monk, who re-founded Whitby as a monastic community – as told by Symeon of Durham (see Day 5). As with many of these old tales the details are sketchy and sometimes confusing, but this is the main outline.

Reinfrid fought with William the Conqueror at the battle of Hastings, and was part of the army of 1069 that harried the north. During this time he had the chance to visit the monastic ruins at Whitby, on its dramatic cliff-top. Reinfrid must have been deeply affected by all he had taken part in, for within a year he had become a monk at Evesham, under the English abbot Aethelwig. Reinfrid then encountered refugees from the north, who had fled from the destruction, for they were given shelter at Evesham.

At this time Aldwin, the prior at the nearby abbey of Winchcombe, was reading Bede's history, and this led Aldwin, Reinfrid and another English monk, Aelfwig (also of Evesham), to journey northwards around 1073/4. They first went to Monkchester, Newcastle, but found it entirely deserted; then they had permission from Bishop Walcher of Durham to settle at Jarrow. But everywhere they went, they found only roofless walls at the great sites, apparently because of continued pirate raids. So at Jarrow they erected a roof of rough-hewn timber and thatch over ruined outbuildings. They lived for several years in cold and draughty huts, fasting for long periods in imitation of their predecessors, as they had read in Bede.

They began to gain recruits; as they grew in number, Aldwin went to try the solitary life at Melrose, where Cuthbert had come from, whilst around 1077 Reinfrid went as a hermit to Whitby, where he had had his first calling. Although he went as a hermit, a community developed around him. Work was begun on a new church building, and a Benedictine community formed. After encouraging the new community for nine years Reinfrid died whilst helping to build a bridge.

Here was a man who was called to the religious life in the midst of a most horrific military campaign. His life completely changed direction, and from being an elite warrior he became dedicated to serving God and needy people. His life might encourage us to pray that people engaged in violence in our day will hear God's call to peace.

PLACES

Hartlepool

On the headland above the old harbour at Hartlepool is the site of Hilda's monastery. Most of the site is now occupied by the church dedicated to St Hilda and begun in the late eleventh century. Evidence of Hilda's monastery has been found, including the remains of her nuns; in the church there is even the headstone of a Saxon nun called Hildithryth.

The church has been developed as a visitor centre as well as a place of worship. It puts on excellent films and provides hand-held players so visitors can learn more about the history of this holy site and the growth of Hartlepool.

Whitby Abbey

Whitby Abbey was founded in 657 by Hilda as a royal monastery on behalf of her kinsman Oswy. As we saw, under Hilda the monastery became known as a place of learning and godly living. After Hilda's death in 680 her successor was Aelffled, daughter of King Oswy and his queen Eanfled, a cousin of Hilda. Although having this royal abbess meant that Whitby was still important, its pre-eminent position was lost, and under Cuthbert Lindisfarne recovered its leading position, which it retained before and after his death.

The abbey was destroyed in a Viking raid of 867, and the site was largely deserted until Reinfrid arrived in the eleventh century. Pilgrims then began to return, and a new church was needed in the twelfth century to cope with the numbers. These are the ruins still visible, which survived the Reformation because they were useful to ships entering the harbour.

English Heritage now care for the buildings and provide excellent interpretation boards and audio tours. They are inclined to over-emphasize the importance of the Synod of Whitby (see Appendix), but there is a full and interesting account of the history of the site from the time of Hilda to the present day.

Prayer

Holy God,
You inspired Hilda to build to your glory
and to train women and men in the ways of holy living.

You inspired Reinfrid to abandon violence
and to become a peacemaker.

You inspired countless pilgrims to journey here
and to find your guidance.

Inspire us in our turn,
through the lives of these holy people,
that we might find your direction and live in your light.

Practicalities

St Hilda's Church, Hartlepool

Hartlepool is just off the A19 and is signed from several exits.
On approaching the town take the signs for the headland
in order to reach St Hilda's Church. The church welcomes
visitors both to services and on Saturdays from 2 p.m. to 4 p.m.
throughout the year – also on Wednesdays and Sundays from
2 p.m. to 4 p.m., Easter to September.

Whitby Abbey

Whitby is reached via a scenic road (A171) over the North
York Moors. Whitby is signed off the A19 at the A174. Once
approaching the town follow signs for the abbey, where there is
ample parking.

The abbey is open every day from 10 a.m. to 6 p.m., April
to September; winter opening is more restricted. Refreshments
and toilets are available at the site and in the town.
http://www.english-heritage.org.uk/server/show/nav.17360

Other places

Lastingham: Lastingham is a delightful village on the southern edge of the North York Moors. There is an old church on the site of Cedd's monastery. The present building dates from after the time of the Norman Conquest and includes an inspiring crypt built in the eleventh century over the place where Cedd is believed to have been buried.

http://www.lastinghamchurch.org.uk/

Rievaulx Abbey: Rievaulx Abbey was built by the Cistercian monks in the twelfth century in a secluded valley about 2 miles from the market town of Helmsley. Its most important period spiritually came under its third abbot, Aelred, who wrote a number of important books, including *The Mirror of Charity* and *Spiritual Friendship*. Aelred came from a priestly family that had been based in Durham and Hexham, and so provides a link to other parts of the pilgrimage in this book. Today these are some of the most complete monastic ruins in northern England, a spectacular sight in the deep and narrow valley.

http://www.english-heritage.org.uk/server/show/nav.17256

The Synod of Whitby

A visit to Whitby Abbey inevitably raises questions about the Synod of Whitby in 664. Some authors have suggested that this was the most significant showdown between Roman and Celtic Christianity, a crucial development in Western Christianity. Others downplay its importance and point to more important synods of the era, such as that of Hertford in 673, when Archbishop Theodore brought some order to the church in this country.

So what can be said about the Synod of Whitby?

The main issue was when Easter should be celebrated, as this was said to be causing problems in the royal household, with King Oswy following the Ionan custom and his queen, Eanfled, a daughter of Edwin, following the Roman ways. Remember, Eanfled was one of the children taken by Paulinus to Kent after the death of Edwin. A second issue was the type of monastic tonsure to be used, as Roman and Irish monks followed different traditions.

These were important issues at the time and caused deep tension between the two sides. However, the disagreement should not be seen as a simple 'Romans against Celts' battle, and Whitby itself was not of huge international significance. The three central points underlying this assertion are:

1. *This was a regional synod, not a national one.*
The synod was chaired not by a bishop but by King Oswy. This was essentially a regional gathering for Oswy's kingdom

of Northumbria. Oswy was bretwalda (high king), so it could be seen to have wider implications for other parts of Britain: some bishops from Wessex and Essex as well as Northumbria were present, but the Archbishop of Canterbury and other bishops were absent. Officially the senior figure on the Roman side was Bishop Agilbert, now Bishop of Paris but familiar with the British scene having been Bishop of Dorchester. In practice Wilfrid – still a priest – with his eloquence and command of the language, was given the honour of leading the speeches for the Roman side. This indicates the ability of Wilfrid, but also that the synod required the views of its regional church leaders. The Irish side of the argument was led by Colman, the Abbot and Bishop of Lindisfarne.

Both appealed to wider practice – Wilfrid to the role of Peter and the practice of the church in Rome and around the Mediterranean, and Colman to the tradition of Columba and through him to St John the Evangelist. The religious arguments were based on the idea that this regional church should follow the wider practice of the church, which takes us to the second point.

2. *Despite Wilfrid's claim, the Western church was not then a unified body in the way it became in the later Middle Ages.*
There were many regional variations in religious practice, of which the Irish customs were just one example. For example, in Francia the unusual practice of double monasteries for men and women had grown up, and throughout Western Europe bishops were able to vary the details of the liturgy for the Mass to a surprising extent. Thus the 'Roman' side was not as united in all things as Wilfrid's rhetoric suggested.

Similarly the 'Celtic' side was not a united body either. There were distinctive features to the church in Ireland, such as their form of monasticism and a strong emphasis on severe penances. But there was no 'Celtic church' in any meaningful sense, for the churches in the lands we think of as Celtic varied amongst themselves and there were no 'Celtic synods' to agree on religious practice.

So there were no straightforward 'Roman' and 'Celtic' churches to have this 'battle'. Leaders such as Columba, Aidan and Cuthbert knew that the Bishop of Rome held a certain pre-eminence, and they all celebrated Mass and said the monastic prayers in Latin, knowing that this was the language of the church. People such as Hilda and Cuthbert drew on both Roman and Irish practices; what may colour our understanding is the sense that they, and perhaps Bede, were unsympathetic to Wilfrid's blunt approach, even if they ultimately agreed with his arguments.

3. *There were important political factors behind the synod as well as religious ones.*
It seems likely that Oswy had already decided his own view before calling the synod, for he had political reasons in favouring a decision for the Roman customs. Amongst them were:

• His intention that his own foundation of Whitby should eclipse Lindisfarne.

• The manoeuvring for power between Oswy and his son Alchfrith, who was the sub-king of Deira, in which Whitby was situated, without going to war.

• Oswy was now dominant in the far north of Scotland, and he may have felt able to impose his will on the Ionan monasteries that were powerful in that area.

There is another factor suggesting that the date of Easter was not the main issue: Oswy and Eanfled had been married for over twenty years and Eanfled was a patroness of Holy Island, despite its different customs. They had coped throughout that time with differing dates for Easter. No wonder a recent historian has claimed, 'It was not the Easter controversy which required prompt attention but the ever changing political situation' (Nick Higham, *The Convert Kings*, p.256).

For these reasons the synod is not as crucial for Western Christianity as some have claimed. It was significant for northern England, but it was part of a wider development, as different regions responded over the course of a century to changes emanating from Rome. In southern Ireland a synod resolved to follow Continental practice as early as 634; in Northumbria it was at Whitby in 664, and then northern Ireland in the 690s, Pictland in the 710s, Iona in the late 720s, and Wales c. 755, perhaps later in south Wales. This list demonstrates that there was no unified 'Celtic church' with one pattern and practice, and that there was real variation amongst places and at different times. The Synod of Whitby was one event in a bigger process of change, and inevitable if regional churches were to keep their sense of belonging to the universal church.

FURTHER READING

Main sources:

Bede, *Ecclesiastical History of the English People*, translated by Leo Sherley-Price (Harmondsworth: Penguin Books, 1990)

Various authors, *The Age of Bede,* translated by J. F. Webb and D. H. Farmer (Harmondsworth: Penguin Books, 1998). This includes Bede's *Life of Cuthbert* and *The Life of Wilfrid* by Eddius Stephanus.

David Rollason (ed.), *Symeon of Durham* (Oxford: OUP, 2000)

John Wesley, *Journals* (Chicago: Moody Press, 1951); these are best found online at: *http://www.ccel.org/ccel/wesley/journal.html*

Popular versions of the stories told by Bede can be found in the many books of David Adam, former vicar of Holy Island, including *The Edge of Glory: Prayers in the Celtic Tradition* (London: Triangle/SPCK, 1985); *Tides and Seasons: Modern Prayers in the Celtic Tradition* (London: Triangle/SPCK, 1989); and *Walking the Edges: Living in the Presence of God* (London: Triangle/SPCK, 2003).

The reflections of Basil Hume in *Footsteps of the Northern Saints* (London: DLT, 1996 and reprinted) remain inspirational.

Other books that are mentioned or that will take you further:

Michelle Brown, *How Christianity Came to Britain and Ireland* (Oxford: Lion Hudson, 2006)

N. J. Higham, *The Convert Kings: Power and Religious Affiliation in Early Anglo-Saxon England* (Manchester and New York: Manchester University Press, 1997)

Helen Julian CSF, *The Lindisfarne Icon: St Cuthbert and the 21st Century Christian* (Oxford: Bible Reading Fellowship, 2004)

Fay Sampson, *Visions and Voyages: The Story of Celtic Spirituality* (Oxford: Lion Hudson, 2007)

Gavin Wakefield, *Alexander Boddy: Pentecostal Anglican Pioneer* (Milton Keynes: Authentic Media, Paternoster Press, 2007)

Benedicta Ward, *The Venerable Bede* (London: Geoffrey Chapman, 1998)